A Baker's Dozen
Chichester's Lost Retailers

Here is God's plenty

Dryden (1700),
commenting on the rich variety of
human endeavour and personality

A Baker's Dozen
Chichester's Lost Retailers

with illustrations by
David Pratt

Edited by
Paul Foster and Sheila Hale

Otter Memorial Paper Number Twenty-nine
University of Chichester
2011

*For Chichester's independent retailers,
yesterday and today*

CONTENTS

Telegrams—FIELD, "CITY MEWS," Chichester.
Telephone No. 193.

City Mews, South Gate, Chichester,

June 1914

Mr J. Shippam

Dr. to MESSRS. FIELD,

Landaus, Waggonettes, Dog Carts,
Phaetons, Brakes, Broughams. . .

Riding and Job Masters,

Single or Pair Horse Wedding Carriages
:: &c. ::

PRIVATE HUNTING AND LIVERY STABLES.
Orders by post promptly attended to.

Dealers in Horses. . . .

Horses carefully shod by competent Smiths.

MOTOR CABS.

£ s d

1914				£	s	d
April 13	To Landau			12	·	
20	" "	Funtington		6	·	
	" Cab	to 30 Southgate		·	1	6
28	" Landau	Lavant & Goodwood		5	·	
May 14	" "	Stoke, Ashling & Fishbourne		5	·	
15	" Brougham	Pilly Green & Race Hill		10	·	
20	" Landau	Goodwood, Lavant & Valdoe		6	·	
21	" "	Bognor & return		12	6	
June 1	" "	Race Hill & Lavant		10	·	
13	" "	Lavant & Goodwood		6	·	
				3	14	·
April 11		By Cash		1	·	·
				£2	14	·

CITY MEWS, CHICHESTER.
No. 832 *Sept 4* 191 4
RECEIVED *By Cash*
per
WITH THANKS
Messrs. FIELD.
£ 2 : 14 :

Messrs Field (Thomas, and later his sons) were horse dealers and jobmasters – people who kept a livery stable and hired out horses/ carriages per job. They owned land off the Oving Road which was sold for building in the 1930s, as well as the City Mews at 'South Gate'. With the growth of the car, the firm became automobile engineers at 31-32 South Street, and later main agents for Austin.
(Courtesy John Shippam)

INTRODUCTION

This book records a slice of cultural history: the loss from Chichester of many independent shops that once flourished in the city. In several instances, such shops, carefully tended by several generations, had successfully traded for almost a century; and some, for much longer still. But times change, and in the past twenty to thirty years the city has lost retailers that once seemed permanent features of the city's streets.

Comment on this change, from a city-scene full of privately-owned shops to a city dominated by multi-nationals, by coffee-shops and other leisure outlets (especially clothing firms) – to the total exclusion of any independent butchers, grocers or greengrocers, will be pursued below; but let's first begin by thinking about Chichester almost 100 years ago. Electric street lighting had only just arrived, each lamp being switched on and off daily by a lamp-lighter; main sewers through the streets had been dug scarcely a decade earlier; local travel was mainly by horse or shank's pony – although the first bicycles were appearing and one could take the 'Hundred of Manhood & Selsey Tram' down to the coast; the first cinema, Poole's Picture Palace in the Corn Exchange, had only just opened (1910), as had the Chichester High Schools – the Girls School the same year (1910), the Boys two years earlier (1908); and the city's population was scarcely 10,000. And nationally, Edward the VII had only just died (1910); a Liberal (Asquith) was leading the government; Emily Davison, the militant suffragette, had yet to be felled and die from the injuries she sustained at Tattenham Corner from the King's horse, Anwer; and thought of the Great War and the tragic loss of life in the trenches was in no-one's mind.

In sum, the Edwardian era was in full swing: the dark and gloom of Victorian England was beginning to dissipate, and Chichester could provide its own pleasures – down to the coast for some, and for others trips up to the Downs, an extant account from the City Mews in Southgate recording in summer 1914 a landau (sometimes a brougham) to places such as Goodwood, Lavant, Pilly Green and Race Hill – see account opposite.

And the Edwardians certainly knew how to celebrate: the 1913 display of Christmas poultry at Kimbell's in East Street (page 42 below) is quite staggering; and the advertising poster of a similar date used by Shippams (see page 11) retains its appeal even today. Scrutiny of *The Official Guide to Chichester* for the period (published by W. H. Barrett of The Cross, Chichester) reveals the city advertising itself as 'an ideal place for any one seeking a healthy quiet old City wherein to reside, or to spend a pleasant holiday [since] the streets are lined with high-class shops'. In support of the claim, the *Guide*, which is forty-two pages long, includes full page advertisements from twelve firms, several of whom will be known to present readers, the best-remembered perhaps being: Hooper & Son - the florists; Charlie Howard – the family butcher; Adcock's Garage – with the shop in North Street, Adcock Printer, specializing in stationery and printing; William Kimbell – baker, confectioner, and tea room proprietor; and Sidney Bastow – the chemist and optician. Less easily remembered may be: W. P. Breach – wine merchant of East Street, or E. F. Saunders – tools, fishing tackle, guns, and cutlery of South Street.

This issue, of memorability, has great significance in the retail world. Good memories – of excellent service, for instance – encourage customers to return; bad memories often do the reverse. At the core of this distinction lies reliability – not just of service, but of product also. And linked to both is the broader quality of loyalty, loyalty from the customer to a particular shop being paralleled by the loyalty and good faith of the proprietors to the customer – across a whole range of values, the courtesy of staff (often including acceptable banter), together with knowledge of their particular trade, being as important as the integrity of pricing and the quality of goods sold.

It is values such as these, along with a family's settled determination, stamina, and willingness to work long hours, that enabled many traditional firms to survive not just for two or three generations, or even for a century, but in some instances much longer: for instance, Byerley & Co. flourished from 1870 to 1984; Faith, the jewellers, from 1833 to 1978 (and from 1823 if one counts their earlier shop in Somerstown); Moore of the later Moore & Tillyer, stationers, from 1880 to 1996; Smurthwaite, the decorators' merchant, from 1857 to 1980; and Arthur Purchase & Son, wine merchants, from at least 1891 to 2007. What is notable about such a brief selection is the variety of business, and it is clear that the endurance of a business for a century or thereabouts (for which period many more firms that feature later in this volume could be cited) is not closely correlated with any particular trade – although it may be significant that two local firms who are still thriving and who have recently celebrated a century of trading (Whitmore Jones at Oving Road, and Andrew McDowall's of North Street) have businesses focussed on clothing or furnishing, as does Richard Doman Furnishing of Stirling Road, which can be traced back to the high Victorian period – 1868.

And yet, further thought shows that the durability of firms specializing in clothing and furnishing is, indeed, related to their specialist products. The closures that this volume records are primarily grouped in a period centring on the 1980s, and it is within that decade that the greatest influence of the arrival in Chichester of the multi-national supermarket can be traced. Admittedly, the city centre Tesco arrived in East Street as early as 1959 (at the site currently occupied by HMV) and, swiftly afterwards, Sainsbury at 15 North Street (currently Santander, the former Abbey National) in October 1961. But these arrivals, of themselves, specializing as they did solely in groceries, were not the crucial factor that led to the closure of so many independent firms. Of far greater influence was the opportunity seized by freehold landlords to profit from the increasing competition (and deep pockets of the multi-nationals) by raising rents – one independent trader featured later in this book noting that the rent demand increased in a single year by well over 300%. Allied to such financial imperatives (including significant increases in business rates) was the development by the multi-nationals of out-of-town supermarkets offering much more than just food, but electrical goods, books and stationery, clothing, pharmacies, pet foods and so on – all accessible from a spacious car-park that is free; and, of course, because of bulk buying, offering astonishingly competitive pricing.

Inevitably, the pressures created by these developments led to the demise of many well-loved firms, and to the creation of a city shopping experience that (today) is little removed from that available in many other cities and towns across the country. In that sense, this volume is an exercise in nostalgia, its thirteen chapters offering a sequence of reminiscence - of 'times past'. In offering that opportunity, the editors and writers are very aware that some readers will cavil at the choices made and be surprised at the omission of a particular trade or shop. But that, together with the variety of treatment, chapter by chapter, of each chosen theme, is seen by the editors as a necessary intention, for it echoes the individuality of Chichester's historic shopping experience – and as such is something to be celebrated.

Across the past 25-30 years, the span of a generation, our retail experience has dramatically changed; and we have lived through a cultural upheaval that has generated profound changes, not just to our own daily and weekly behaviour, but also to that of many public bodies as well. At the present time, there are, within the centre of Chichester, almost fifty establishments where one can enjoy a coffee or tea – along with an hour or so wandering past or through one clothing shop after another. Such is this omnipresence (of coffee and clothes) that the city centre might be characterized as no longer a working city but rather as having become a city of leisure. Such an idea may be feasible, and successful, but it would be more reassuring if we were able to welcome to our streets a much greater individuality.

In some cities, there have been appearing what are termed 'concept' stores, stores that offer – on quite a small scale – a surprise: kilims from Turkey alongside wall-hangings from India, together with hand-crafted books and tins of Alaskan Amber; or a shop with panels of stained glass, pots of mignonette, leather wall panels decorated with shells, clothes by a new (local) designer and, in accord with today's environmental concerns, several stylish bicycles together, perhaps, with a classic car. What pleasure that kind of development would provide – not just for the shopper, but for the retailers themselves: it would require creative endeavour of the most significant kind, of the kind that enlarges one's horizon and nourishes the soul. But that, in turn, is something that can be shared: just as many of the independent proprietors of shops that feature in this volume created, from the 1930s through, say, to the 1970s, a shared civic community at the very core of city life, so a new understanding of retail possibilities could contribute strongly to creating an individuality and cohesion that could lift the spirit of all who are associated with this distinguished city.

* * * * *

Preparation of a book of this kind relies on assistance from many different sources, and it is with deep appreciation that we record here the skills and contribution of the many writers - without whom this publication would scarcely have been possible. For them, as for the editors, there has been a heavy dependence on the archival resources at the West Sussex Record Office. Led by Alan Readman (County Archivist), and Alison McCann (who has a special responsibility for archives relating to Chichester), staff there have willingly guided writers to many resources without which several of the various chapters would be lacking crucial historical data: of particular relevance has been the series of various Directories for Chichester which run fairly successively from 1797 to 1974; the large archive of photographs relating to Chichester; copies of *Chichester Observer*; rate books; electoral rolls; Goad maps;* local history books and other similar publications. Of importance, also, has been the assistance provided by staff at the Chichester District Museum, particularly for photographs from their collections.

Over and above these formal resources has been the help received from friends and acquaintances** who, when asked about some of Chichester's former independent shops, have readily shared their memories and, in several cases, prompted lines of enquiry that would otherwise have been overlooked. In a number of instances, the information provided has been of historical importance to this publication and the relevant personal appreciation is included at the end of each chapter, as are reference data for specific documents that writers have cited or found especially illuminating. As regards resources available on the internet, the following sites have proved useful: www.prtsoc.org.uk [site of the Parish Register Transcription Society]; www.westsussexpast.org.uk/searchonline (Record Office Catalogue); www.findmypast.com; www.ancestry.co.uk; Wikipedia (although some entries need to be treated with considerable caution, and many are incomplete); and the *Oxford Dictionary of National Biography*.

Publication would not have been possible without grant assistance from the Bassil Shippam and Alsford Trust, from Guardian Stockbrokers (of City Road, London), and from the City Council, to whom we extend particular thanks. For agreement to host the launch of the volume in the Assembly Room at The Council House, we are in debt to the Mayor of Chichester, Councillor Tony French, and to the assistance of City Council staff, led by the Town Clerk, Rodney Duggua. On a more personal note, we conclude by recording here the unfailing courtesy extended by Tom Hale to one of the joint editors over the entire eighteen months this volume has been in preparation, together with his tolerant and enduring forbearance over a similar period to the other joint editor.

Paul Foster   Sheila Hale

October   2011

* Named after Chas E. Goad (1878-1970) who produced the first detailed street maps that incorporated individual buildings and their uses.
** Sadly three, who were keenly enthusiastic about the project, have died before completion – they are Jenny Pine, Nigel Purchase, and Vivian Meynell.

1
Bread and Confectionery

Frances Lansley

Bread is worth all, being the Staffe of life.
(J. Penkethman, 1638)

The aroma of freshly baked bread is the most evocative of smells. Today, most of us buy bread from supermarkets, usually sliced and ready wrapped and made in vast bread factories. Supermarkets know how enticing the smell of bread is in making anonymous aisles friendly and welcoming, reminding customers of a cosier past. In-store 'bakeries' ensure the smell of fresh bread lingers around the store.

But in the early 1950s nearly all bread was still bought at a local bakery, where the bread was usually baked on the premises. Bakeries were so numerous and important in this period that they were found not just in town centres, but also in most suburbs and villages. Chichester had two bakeries in the Somerstown area, as well as bakeries in Whyke, St Pancras, the Hornet and Orchard Street. Fishbourne managed to support two bakeries, and many other villages in the surrounding area, including Bosham and Sidlesham, also had their own bakeries. Bakeries in the centre of Chichester in 1950 included J Atkins at 70 North Street, Devonia Bakery at 13 Southgate, Rogers at 15 East Street and 12 St Martin's Street, Spurriers at 70/71 South Street, and A B West at 11 Little London. Bakeries just outside the centre included Furneaux Bakery at 14 St Pancras, William Voke at 108 the Hornet, and A G Udell at 161 Orchard Street.

Many bakers, such as William and Laurie Kimbell, specialised in confectionery, producing wonderful cakes and sweets. Some bakers opened cafés and restaurants on their premises. In the case of Chichester, the Voke family of bakers ran a tea garden in The Hornet before the Second World War, the Smith family ran cafés in West Street and East Street, the Kimbells had a restaurant (the House of Kimbell) in North Street, and the Spurriers had a café at their bakery in South Street. Bakers, such as the Kimbells and Smiths, also offered outside catering, providing food for big functions and events.

In the 1950s a large proportion of the population lived within easy walking distance of a bakery, and children enjoyed being sent to buy bread, nibbling warm crusts on the walk home. Children also appreciated the bakeries on school days: boys at Chichester Central School (situated in New Park Road until the 1960s) enjoyed buying lardy cakes at the Furneaux Bakery in St Pancras, and children at the Lancastrian Schools warmed themselves by the wall of Udell's Bakery in Orchard Street. Most bakers also offered a delivery service, and the baker's van was a comforting sight. A large number of 'roundsmen' were employed to deliver the bread, using horses and carts in the early years of the twentieth century before motorised vehicles were introduced.

But not everything was perfect. A letter in the *Chichester Observer* of 1915 complained: 'In these days of germs and microbes, flies and dustbins, can anything be done to induce or compel the local bakers to carry their bread inside their carts? It is the usual practice to carry some of it outside on the top of the carts and hand trucks, exposed to all weathers, flies, etc. Is not this a danger to public health, especially in dry and windy weather when the bread is covered by road dust?' Bread delivered in this way does not sound very appetising!

Hygiene and health and safety requirements were often quite lax by today's standards. Before the First World War, William Kimbell had the stables for his horses at the back of his new bakehouse in St Martin's Street and horses were taken back and forth through the area where bread was being baked. The horses always wanted to linger in the bakery, possibly due to the warmth. When he took over a bakery in Southsea in the 1920s, he discovered that it was full of large and terrifying rats and cockroaches. All sorts of measures were tried in a desperate attempt to get rid of the vermin, including using a dog and traps, and it took weeks to solve the problem.

The work of the bakers and confectioners changed as the twentieth century progressed. Gas ovens replaced the old wood and coal burning ovens and were cleaner and easier to use, producing more even results. The increasing mechanisation of baking from the late nineteenth century onwards also had a major impact on the small local bakers, and eventually contributed to their demise. A significant change in the way bread was produced and sold happened with the introduction of bread slicing and wrapping machines. In America, Otto Rohwedder had started work on developing a bread slicing machine before the First World War, although it was not until 1928 that his invention was first exhibited at a bakery trade fair in America.* Within just a few years nearly all bread in the United States was sold pre-sliced and wrapped, and the expression 'the best thing since sliced bread' was coined. In Britain the slicing and wrapping of loaves was prohibited during the Second World War as an economy measure, but reintroduced in 1950.

By the mid 1960s the number of independent bakers was beginning to fall quite dramatically, with more bread being produced on an industrial scale and sold in supermarkets. Local bakers could not compete with the cheap prices at which bread was sold in supermarkets. Yet, not only was large scale production impacting on local bakers: British people were eating less bread as the century progressed, and by 2000, British people were eating about half the amount of bread per person that they had been eating in 1950. By the late twentieth century the number of local bakeries had declined enormously. Bread made locally is still available, but is becoming more

* [Sliced bread was first sold the same year by the Chillicothe Baking Company in Missouri. *Eds*]

upmarket and expensive, produced, for example, at bakeries attached to 'farm shops' or by specialist rural bakeries, rather than in the city.

Five of the most prominent families of bakers and confectioners in Chichester in the mid twentieth century were the Kimbells, Vokes, Rogers, Spurriers and Smiths.

LAURIE KIMBELL, 21 North Street

During WW2 and the post-war years of austerity, the citizens of Chichester would frequent The House of Kimbell, one of the best-known local venues for relaxation and entertainment between 1940 and 1954. The House included not only a café and restaurant, but also a dance hall and bakery, and became a popular venue for a simple pot of tea and cake during the day, and for glamorous dinner-dances in the evening. These grand premises at 21 North Street were specially built for Laurie Kimbell, but are now occupied by Marks & Spencer.

A surviving tea menu includes items now rarely seen, such as 'scotch woodcock' (scrambled eggs on toast with anchovy paste) and 'herring roes on toast'. Items still popular today also included baked beans on toast, scones, fancy cakes, and cream meringues. Coffee was just served as 'black or white'! Numerous private and civic functions were held at the premises, including meetings of the Rotary Club and the West Sussex Catenian Association.

The House of Kimbell was owned by Laurie (Lawrence) Kimbell and was founded by Laurie and his father, William Kimbell, in 1939. The Kimbell family had managed bakeries in the Chichester area since the 19th century, when the family moved south from Oxfordshire (another branch of the family became grocers in East Street). William Kimbell's father, Frank (Francis) Kimbell, was born in the hamlet of Fencott near Bicester, the son of baker and grocer Thomas Kimbell and his wife Rosanna. By 1871 the family lived in Chichester where William Kimbell was born in 1880. By this time his father, Frank Kimbell, had a small bakery in St Pancras, and was also a corn dealer.

West Sussex Record Office has a copy of a memoir William Kimbell wrote in 1946, giving insight into a baker's and confectioner's early life and career, demanding tenacious dedication and long working hours. When William was only six, his family moved from St Pancras to Birdham where they lived for about five years before moving back to Chichester. William left school at 13 to work in his father's Chichester bakery. When 17, he was sent to London to gain experience in another bakery at Westminster. He became so tired that he often fell asleep fully clothed at the end of the day! After just 18 months in London, William Kimbell got another job at a bakery in Southsea before returning to the Westminster bakery. His father then asked him to return to Chichester and take charge of the confectionery in the bakery and confectionary shop the family now owned at 13 Southgate. The 1901 Census lists both William (then aged

21) and his older brother Charles (aged 22) working at their father's bakery: William as 'confectioner' and Charles as 'baker – breadmaker'. Their younger sister, Jessie (aged 14), was described as 'assistant baker' and probably helped in the shop. Two older children, Annie and Robert, had been working in the bakery and shop at the time of the 1891 Census, but had probably left home by 1901. A younger sister, Constance, was still at school in 1901.

At the Dolphin Hotel in Chichester, William Kimbell met and fell in love with Daisy Knightly, a hotel employee. They married in 1904. Their marriage was long and, apparently, very happy. Daisy was from Portsmouth, and also the daughter of a baker. Two children were born: Laurie in 1905 and Doris in 1910. A great sadness followed the death of Doris from meningitis in 1926 at the young age of 16.

In 1902 Frank Kimbell opened a confectionary shop and restaurant at 15 East Street (on the corner of St Martin's Street) and, after his marriage to Daisy, William Kimbell bought this business from his father, paying him back in instalments. He also bought the premises formerly occupied by the King's Arms Inn at 12 St Martin's Street and converted it into a bakery, installing new steam ovens. The shop at 15 East Street is now occupied by Clintons Cards and 12 St Martin's Street is used by Marks & Spencer for delivery bays.

William and Daisy's early married life was filled with unremitting hard work with hardly any time for leisure. They lived above the shop in East Street, which was so unsanitary that Daisy got diphtheria after the birth of Laurie in 1905. They built up the business in Chichester, with the help of William's younger sister Connie and, in addition to the bakery, also provided catering for garden parties, mayoral banquets, and Hunt Balls. The parties were huge, often involving hundreds of guests. With no bread-slicing machines, all the bread had to be sliced by hand. William Kimbell took great pride in his decorative confectionery, and began showing his handiwork in different exhibitions, winning prizes (see page 21). In 1913 the family left Chichester and moved to Bognor Regis for Daisy's health, and for a time they ran a bakery there.

The First World War was a very difficult time for bakers as it was hard to get staff, and impossible to get decent flour. No bread could be sold unless it was at least twelve hours old in an attempt to avoid wastage. William Kimbell notes in his autobiography: 'I used to start work at 5am making confectionery all the day and then spend the evening and night up to 10 or 11 o'clock baking bread ready for next day'. In addition, he had to do training with the local fire brigade and guard duty at Ford railway station!

This all got too much for him: he decided to sell the business and join the army as a cook. William didn't sign the papers when he found he would have to go to Italy, and instead the family moved to Tunbridge Wells in Kent, starting a new business including a bakery shop and a restaurant. But Daisy was homesick for Southsea, and so they decided to return to Southsea and start all over again. They bought premises near the Queen's Hotel and the whole family (including Laurie and Doris, before her death in

CHICHESTER <u>The Favourite Tea Room Resort.</u>

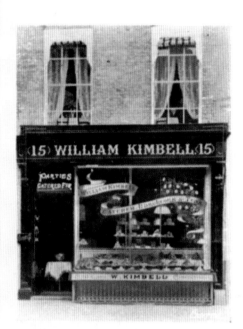

William Kimbell

15, East Street

Dainty Teas and Light Refreshments

served in first-class style.

MODERATE CHARGES.

BRIDE CAKE SPECIALIST.

Caterer for Balls, Suppers, Wedding Receptions and Garden Parties.

HYGIENIC STEAM BAKERY:

12, St. Martin's, Chichester.

Fig.1. Advertisement from City Guide *(W.H. Barrett, c.1911)*

17

1926) worked hard to build up the business, which included a bakery and restaurant. Their business expanded, and rooms at the rear of the premises were converted into a large space for functions, wedding receptions, and dances. The business continued to grow with additional premises being taken over. William Kimbell was successful enough to buy some land in Bedhampton and built a fine new house for his family, which was called St Gyles.

Laurie Kimbell grew up with the bakery and confectionary business in his blood, and he began to help in his parent's business as soon as he was old enough. He was interested in the artistic decoration of wedding cakes, and his father arranged for him to spend some time with a baker and confectioner in Cowes on the Isle of Wight, to increase his experience. Laurie then joined the Cadena Company in Cheltenham, and also spent some time in Tunbridge Wells before returning to work with his father. Laurie was especially interested in exhibition work, and began winning medals and cups at Bakers' and Confectioners' exhibitions.

The business in Southsea eventually grew too large for William Kimbell to be happy and he suffered from nervous exhaustion. In 1937 he went on a long trip by himself to Australia to visit his older brothers, who had emigrated there. Laurie was left in charge of the business with an under-manager. When William returned

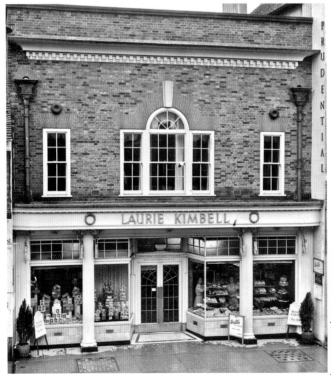

Fig. 2. "House of Kimbell" at 21 North Street (now part of Marks & Spencer); see also the enlarged rain hoppers, sporting on the right hopper, LK (Laurence Kimbell) and the opening date, 1939, and on the left hopper PWM for Panell, William and Mary. William Pannell was a 'mealman', a trader in meal (flour); he married Mary Stevens in 1710 and a conveyance of 1732 reveals his negotiating 21 North Street from a John Farhill.

home, he was back in full health, but the business had become so big and impersonal that neither he nor Laurie wanted to continue working there. Under the terms of their contract with the company (now known as Brickwoods), they could not start a new business in Portsmouth, and so they decided to make a fresh start in Chichester.

In 1939 the Kimbells began planning their new premises in Chichester. The plans submitted to Chichester City Council in July 1939 were for a magnificent new building, including a shop, café and dance hall. The builders were Hood and Taylor of Horsham, and the architect was Harry Osborn of 45 North Street, Chichester. The work involved the demolition of old buildings in both North Street and Chapel Street. The original plan has survived and shows the scale of the enterprise. Entering from North Street, there was first a shop area and, beyond this, a foyer with a fountain and telephone. Beyond the foyer was a large restaurant and ballroom, with a stage for an orchestra at the far end, and a service corridor running down the side. Behind the ballroom was the kitchen and, at the very back, approached by a passage from the kitchen lined with storerooms and scullery, was the bakery itself, including a decorating room, ovens and bakery store. The first floor had a private luncheon room at the front, and then balconies with balustrades encircling the restaurant and ballroom, and leading to cloakrooms and offices at the back of the building. The grandest feature was a magnificent curved staircase at the end of the restaurant. The stairs were like something from a Hollywood film or a cruise ship, and swept up on both sides of the orchestra to a half-landing, with more stairs leading up to the balconies. And then, above the stairs, a beautiful arched window faced west towards Chapel Street.

Fig. 3. Interior of Kimbells

The plans could not have been submitted at a worse time. Britain was on the cusp of the Second World War and, by the time they had been approved in September 1939, war had been declared. The war caused delays in completing the building, with a shortage of construction men and materials, and the stress made Laurie unwell. However, the Kimbells managed to open the building in Easter 1940, with Daisy supervising the shop. Mrs Burt was engaged as manageress with twelve waitresses, a chef, and kitchen staff. The opening was promoted by advertisements in the *Chichester Observer* with the slogan 'Meet me at the House of Kimbell'. By July 1940 tea dances were being advertised every Thursday from 4 to 6 pm and supper dances every Wednesday from 8 to 12 pm. The advertisements drew attention to the 'sprung maple floor' and the free car park (obviously considered important even in 1940).

Initially, the business was run by William and Daisy, while Laurie joined the army and became a Captain in the Catering Department, based at Hilsea Barracks. Laurie married Millicent Wright in Wolverhampton in 1941. Life was not easy with the air raids, but soon people were queuing to buy bread, cakes and confectionery. When the terrible air raid of February 1943 took place, Kimbells was packed, but although the bakery was damaged, no one in the building was killed. When the war ended, Laurie and Millicent moved to a house called Greenwood in Fishbourne Road, Chichester, and took over the running of the business. William and Daisy spent their retirement at their house in Bedhampton. William died in November 1959, and Daisy at the age of 86 in 1965.

Fig. 4. Laurie Kimbell and his wife, Millicent, with their daughter, Carole (c. 1954)

On 11 September 1954 the House of Kimbell closed and John Perring (home furnishers) moved into the premises. An article in the *Chichester Observer* of 13 August 1954 announcing the closure quoted Laurie Kimbell as saying, 'It has all happened very suddenly … My immediate plans after the sale of the equipment will be to have a holiday. I shall be sorry in many ways to sever my business connexions with the city but I hope to continue to reside here'. It was noted that Laurie Kimbell had won '50 Gold Medals and many other awards for confectionery and cooking on the continent as well as in this country'.

Fig. 5. Two examples of the Kimbells' remarkable skill in sugar confectionery: 'Defiance' won a Gold Medal at the International Confectioners' Exhibition, London (1928); the cake was a special commission in 1932 for the Golden Wedding of Sir John and Lady Timpson (Lord and Lady Mayoress of Portsmouth)

ROGERS, 15 East Street

The premises at 15 East Street and the steam bakery 12 St Martin's Street, which had been used by William Kimbell before the First World War, were taken over by J Wickham and Son in the 1920s. Wickhams advertised themselves as 'high-class bakers, confectioners and caterers' and also offered lunches and 'dainty teas'. T H Fuller & Son took over the premises for a brief period at the beginning of the 1930s and they were followed, in 1932, by Arthur William and Louisa Alice Rogers. Rogers Bakery became a well-known business in Chichester during the following couple of decades. The Chichester City Valuation List of 1934 lists Arthur William Rogers as the occupier of 15 East Street, although the building was owned by A Ridley Bax. Mr

Fig. 6. Rogers shop front in East Street

and Mrs Rogers appear, like the Kimbells before them, to have originally lived above the premises at 15 East Street. By 1939, however, they had moved to a house in a more residential area, 11 Laburnum Grove, and they lived there for the next ten years before moving to a house in Parklands, where they stayed until their deaths in the early 1960s.

St Martin's Street was one of the streets in the centre of Chichester that was worst affected by the bombs that fell on the City on 10 February 1943. Number 7 St Martin's Street (on the opposite side of the road to the bakehouse) was totally destroyed and its occupants killed. The bakehouse itself was badly damaged and a new bakehouse had to be quickly built in the summer of 1943. The architect was Harry Osborn of North Street, Chichester (also responsible for Kimbell's new building). The three old ovens were saved, and repaired, and re-used in the new bakehouse, which was set further back, so the street could be widened. In addition to the three ovens, the single storey bakehouse included a furnace, a firing space behind the ovens, a fuel store, and a yard and store at the back. There was a chimney with three flues above the ovens.

Sheila Trust, one of the former customers of Rogers, remembers buying currant buns in the 1950s to take back to the office at the furniture store where she worked. Apparently, if you ordered 12 buns you were always given 13 …a true 'baker's dozen'! But the premises at St Martin's were taken over by 1962 by Tip Top Bakeries of Brighton. The premises at 15 East Street continued as a baker's shop for some years, with Acres the Baker taking over in 1969. In the 1960s Marks & Spencer expanded into the bakehouse premises at 12 St Martin's Street, and delivery lorries now move in and out of the area where bread used to be made.

VOKES & SONS, The Hornet

The Vokes were another Chichester family who were well known for their bakery and confectionary products, and especially for the popular tea gardens in The Hornet. The tea gardens closed in 1940, but William Voke continued running a bakery in the Hornet until the 1950s.

Fig. 7. The Voke shop in The Hornet

Henry John Voke and his wife Kate were already running a successful bakery and confectioner's shop at '47 The Hornet' in the opening years of the twentieth century. At the time of the 1901 Census they had two small sons, William and Ernest, and a servant. In 1907 they took over the larger premises next door at '48 The Hornet' and expanded their business by opening a tea garden. The houses in the Hornet were completely renumbered in the 1930s, and Number 48 became 6 The Hornet (next door to the Eastgate Inn). There was great excitement in Chichester when the Vokes opened a tea garden in July 1907. There was a lengthy article in the *Chichester Observer*, which even included photographs of the gardens. The newspaper commented that Mr Voke 'has just made a great development of his business by the provision of a new bakery, shop and premises, and the addition of secluded, spacious and picturesque tea gardens'. A lot of money must have been spent: the fittings were of walnut and marble and there were Japanese curtains dividing the shop. A covered corridor led from the shop to the tea gardens, which were at the rear of the adjoining premises and occupied surprisingly large grounds. The new bakery was apparently fitted with all the latest appliances, including two steam ovens and two continuous ovens capable of turning out 400 loaves every hour. There was a mixer capable of making sufficient dough for 400 loaves every quarter of an hour. In addition to the bakehouse, there was a new 'bread room' from which loaves were checked and passed out to the delivery vans. The coach house and stables for the delivery horses were at the rear. The gardens sounded idyllic, being screened by trees and quite removed from the bustle of the town. Hundreds of people attended the opening ceremony, but unfortunately the weather was not very good, although the rain did not come until the evening. Advertisements for the tea garden promised 'complete seclusion in a sylvan retreat' and a 'restful spot for cyclists'.

Fig. 8. Hornet Tea Gardens 1917

Henry John Voke's father, John Voke, had been a miller at Langstone and Hambrook, and Henry John was also interested in the flour trade, selling both his own self-raising flour and a commodity advertised as 'The Chichester Cake Flour.' Henry John Voke was an influential man in Chichester: in addition to running his business in The Hornet he was a City Councillor in the 1930s. He also appears to have owned some of the land on which the Whyke Estate was subsequently built and which was purchased by the City Council shortly before the War.

Henry John was not the only child of John Voke to run a bakery in Chichester: his older sister, Kate, was also a baker and confectioner in her own right. Both Henry John and Kate learnt the trade working as assistants to George Mant, a baker in North Street. At the time of the 1901 Census, Miss Kate Voke (then aged 31) was listed as running her own bakery and confectionary business at 79 North Street, Chichester.

Fig. 9. Another Voke shop (North Street), previously Mant in George Street, Somerstown

Henry John Voke died in Chichester in 1939 at the age of 68, but his oldest son, William, had by then taken over the business in the Hornet. [Another son, Ernest , ran a fruit shop in North Street]. William was born in 1894 in Chichester and grew up at the bakery premises, training to become a baker like his father. In the First World War he worked in the Army Service Corps and in 1918, at the age of 23, he married Phyllis Anna Nash Lewis in Gloucester. Phyllis Voke was a librarian before her marriage and came originally from Stonehouse near Stroud.

The tea gardens and bakery at 6 The Hornet were closed at the beginning of the Second World War, but William Voke stayed in The Hornet, opening a new bakery at 108 The Hornet, between a butcher's shop and Cedo Tyre Company. Plans were submitted in 1939 for the erection of a new bakery building at the back of an existing shop at 108 The Hornet. The plan, which was approved, shows a small single storey building with an asbestos roof. William Voke took over these premises, running the bakery at this location until [?the late 1950s]. The shop later became Planet Models and Handicrafts.

William and Phyllis Voke moved to a house in Whyke Road and they were still living there when Phyllis Voke died in 1974. William died only three years later in 1977.

Fig. 10. Tudor Café, to the left of the picture

TUDOR CAFÉ (SMITHS), 78 East Street

A family that was well known for their confectionery in Chichester was the Smiths, who owned the Tower and Tudor Cafes. George Leonard Smith and his wife Annie Dora appear to have moved to Chichester from Kent at the end of the First World War. By 1920 they had taken over Cowley's bakery and restaurant at 78 East Street, in premises now occupied by the Early Learning Centre. The business at 78 East Street was first listed under the name 'Tudor Café' in directories of the early 1930s.

The Smiths were successful enough to open another shop and café at 18 West Street in late 1931 or early 1932, in premises previously known as Clifton House. (The building has now been absorbed by the House of Fraser Department Store). George Leonard Smith submitted a plan to Chichester City Council in 1931 for rearrangement of the premises at 18 West Street to form a café. The new café was called the Tower Café (being directly opposite the Bell Tower). At the time of the Chichester City Valuation List of 1934, George Leonard Smith was described as both owner and occupier of the two business premises, 78 East Street and 18 West Street, each of which was listed as including a shop and restaurant. The Smiths lived outside the city centre at a house called Redlands in Lavant Road, Summersdale.

George Leonard Smith died in April 1934, at the relatively young age of 56, and only a few years after the opening of the Tower Café. He was buried at East Lavant and a large number of people attended the funeral service. He was survived by his wife, Annie Dora, and two sons, and they appear to have taken over the running of the businesses, with Murray F Smith eventually managing the Tudor Café.

In December 1934 Annie Dora Smith submitted plans for a new shopfront and interior alterations to 78 East Street, approved by Chichester City Council, although they objected to the projecting pilasters. The architect, Donald Hamilton, was from a firm in London. The premises were described as 'Tudor Café Caterers, Confections'. Mrs Smith was obviously keen to improve the premises, as further plans were submitted in 1935 for alterations to the bakehouse, which was located behind the main part of the building fronting North Pallant (a building later taken over by Perfect Timing). Plans were also submitted in 1940 by 'Tower and Tudor Cafes Ltd' for alterations to the kitchen area at the back of the bakehouse.

The death of Murray Smith resulted in the closure of the Tower Café in September 1956. Murray's younger brother, Alan George Warren Smith, who previously managed the Tower Café, now wanted to concentrate the business on the Tudor Café, which had been managed by Murray Smith before his death. The Tower Café was therefore sold to Morant's Department Store (later taken over by the Army & Navy) and Mr A G W Smith took over the management of the Tudor Café. Morant's wanted to use the building at 18 West Street for their own café, to be known as Morant's Café.

The Tudor Café was still open in 1969 and was advertised in *Kelly's Chichester Directory* of 1970 as 'high class caterers and confectioners'. The business appears to have closed by 1971 when the Singer Sewing Machine Company took over the premises and submitted a planning application for alterations to the building. Rotherdale Ltd applied for permission to use the rear of 78 East Street as offices.

SPURRIERS, 19 North Street, and 70-71 South Street

A bakery firm that was prominent in Chichester in the years between the Second World War and the late 1970s was Spurriers. Spurriers originally had two shops in Chichester: one at 19 North Street and one at 70/71 South Street, near the Market Cross. The shop at 19 North Street is now occupied by Holland & Barrett (Health Foods) and that in South Street by Perfect Timing.

The bakeries on these two sites had previously been owned by Joseph Richard Hobbs, who worked as a baker in Chichester for over fifty years, following in the footsteps of his father who was also a baker. Joseph Hobbs was an important man in Chichester in the first half of the twentieth century for, in addition to running his successful bakery business, he served on Chichester City Council for 43 years, including two years as Mayor in 1920-1922, and he was also a County Councillor. He was 87 when he announced his retirement from local government service in 1954 (he had retired from his bakery business just before the Second World War). Joseph Hobbs, and his wife Annie, were both born in Chichester, and Joseph's father (also called Joseph Hobbs) ran the bakery at 19 North Street, which his son eventually took over. As was then the custom, Joseph and Annie lived near their place of work, first in North Street and later at the bakery premises in South Street. In the late 1930s they moved to a more spacious house called Calloways, in Fishbourne Road. Joseph Hobbs was reputedly famous in the area for introducing the first motorised delivery van for his bakery rounds. Before that he had maintained seven horses to pull his carts.

Unlike Joseph and Annie Hobbs, Albert E Spurrier, his wife Kate and their children were not from Sussex, but moved down from the London area. Alfred Spurrier was born in Bethnal Green in the East End of London in 1893 and ran a successful firm of bakeries in London before the Second World War. He appears to have sold his London shops in 1945 and bought the two bakeries in Chichester, which had previously belonged to Joseph Hobbs.

The Spurriers employed George and Olive Syrett to manage the shops in Chichester. The Syretts had already managed shops for the Spurriers in London, moving down to Chichester in 1945. They lived in a flat above the premises in South Street with

their children and Sheila, their daughter, has vivid memories of moving to Chichester when she was aged 14 and living over the shop in South Street from 1945 to 1955. She remembers how the old building had to be held up by huge props and a steel girder when it was in danger of collapsing into the road due to an invasion of death watch beetle. The flat had been used as an Air Raid Wardens Post in the War and had to be renovated when the Syrett family moved in. The old building was very spooky and Sheila was sure that it was haunted, although probably by a friendly female ghost! Sheila also remembered how four or five men would arrive at 5 am, six days a week, to bake cakes and buns for both shops. Hot Cross Buns were very special, and were only sold on Good Friday.

Fig. 11. Spurriers' premises in South Street after the rebuilding of the entire front wall c. 1949

The premises in South Street had a shop at the front, beyond which was a cosy tearoom. The bakehouse building, with its oven, was situated behind the main building. A new gas oven was installed when alterations were made to modernise the building in 1948.

As far as the shop in North Street was concerned, Sheila remembers this as being a 'funny little shop', bow-fronted, up a step, with the bread bakery behind, and access for it and roundsmen through a yard in Crane Street. The Spurriers placed advertisements in the *Chichester Observer* of 1950 to promote their shops: 'Have you tried the new ideal loaf? Delicious and nutritious – Spurriers of Chichester – our bake houses are open to daily inspection'.

Mr and Mrs Spurrier did not just have bakeries in Chichester: they bought several shops along the Sussex Coast, and there were Spurrier bakeries in Worthing, Lancing, Shoreham and Brighton. The shops were distributed among their many children and in 1955 the Chichester shops were taken over by

Fig. 12. Spurriers' premises in South Street prior to the need for rebuilding – with a very well-stocked window display

Cyril Spurrier and his wife Doreen. Cyril and his wife Doreen did not live near the shops: they lived some miles outside Chichester, at a cottage in Forestside near the Hampshire border. Olive Syrett was a good saleswoman and popular with staff and customers and the shop on South Street was very busy. Sheila Syrett worked in the shop on Saturday mornings when she was in the 6th Form at the Chichester High School for Girls. George and Olive Syrett moved to Brighton for a few years in 1955 to manage the two Spurrier shops there, but in 1958 they returned to Chichester and took over Wakeford's florist and fruiterer's shop that used to be opposite Spurriers.

The Spurriers gave up the premises in North Street in 1958 and concentrated on the shop in South Street. A plan was submitted to change the use of the premises in North Street from a bakery to a dry cleaning unit, but this was refused as being detrimental to neighbouring shops. An application by a firm in Brighton to demolish and rebuild the shop premises was, however, approved in 1959, and the former bakery became a women's clothes shop. Cyril Spurrier appears to have kept the bakery in South Street until about 1979. By May 1980 the bakery had gone, and the Sussex Building Society had moved into the shop.

This was the beginning of a fast-approaching end for Chichester's High Street Bakers. The sweet smell of freshly baked bread warming early morning high street hours would soon become a smell of the past.

CODA: NOTE ON RATIONING

Something that had a big impact on bakers in Chichester was the introduction of bread and flour rationing after the Second World War. The importance the government attached to the baking industry was shown by the fact that bakers were a reserved occupation and not conscripted. Throughout the period of the Second World War bread was one of the few essential items that was never strictly rationed, although there were restrictions on the type of bread produced (with the introduction of a 'national loaf') and people could be prosecuted for wasting bread or feeding it to the birds. The scarcity and poor quality of bread during the First World War had such an adverse impact on people's morale, that the government was determined not to repeat this experience during the Second World War. Only after the war ended and famine threatened many parts of Europe did the government announce the introduction of bread and flour rationing, which was to commence on 21 July 1946. The rationing of bread continued for two years, until July 1948.

The proposed system of rationing was extremely complicated and there were lengthy notices in the *Chichester Observer* advising people about the scheme. The rationing was based on a system of 'Bread Units' (or 'BUs') with a small loaf being two BUs and a large one 4 BUs. Manual male workers had the largest allowance, getting 15 Bread Units a week. Female manual workers and expectant mothers got 11 Bread Units and 'normal' adults only got 9 bread units. Growing adolescents between 11 and 18 were lucky and got 12 Bread Units. Bread Units were also used for cakes and flour (one Bread Unit entitled you to ½ lb of cakes, buns or scones!).

The introduction of bread rationing was very unpopular, and opposed by many bakers, including those in Chichester. The National Association of Master Bakers and Confectioners declared their refusal to operate the scheme, and the Chichester and District Branch held a meeting in July 1946 at which they voted to support the stand of the National Association. Mr J W Atkins was President of the Chichester and District Branch at this time and Mr Murray Smith was Secretary. It was William Voke who proposed the amendment that the Chichester and District Branch should support the stand being taken by the National Association.

The rebellion was short lived, and the Chichester bakers held an emergency meeting on the following Sunday at which they reluctantly decided that they would cooperate after all.

The opposition to rationing made front page news in the *Chichester Observer* of 27 July 1946, with an article stating: "'Absolute chaos', 'roundsmen discontent', 'Roundsman gives his notice' . . . such were Chichester bakers' remarks on Wednesday referring to the start of bread rationing". Bakers were angry about the problems caused by having to handle thousands of coupons, the fact that their delivery men were taking longer to do their rounds, and they were worried that bread sales would decrease. Mr Syrett, manager of Spurriers, was quoted saying, 'One roundsman was not able to complete his calls on Tuesday, mainly because of lack of co-operation from customers ... As to the shop trade, if we go on like this we shall have to do away with two-thirds of the production staff'.

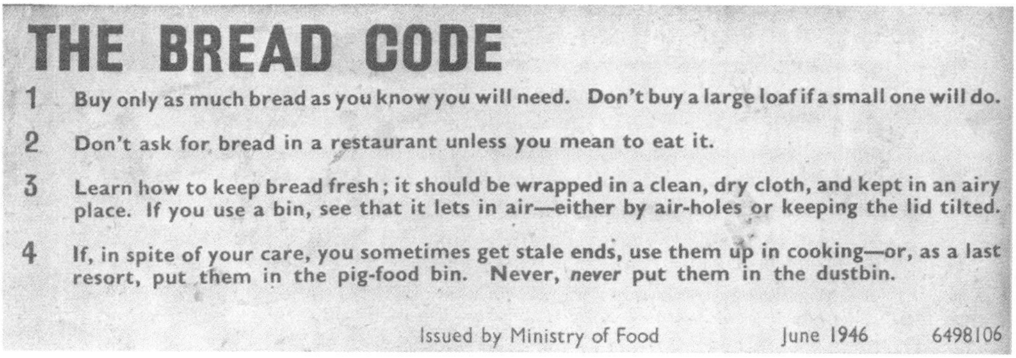

THE BREAD CODE

1   Buy only as much bread as you know you will need. Don't buy a large loaf if a small one will do.

2   Don't ask for bread in a restaurant unless you mean to eat it.

3   Learn how to keep bread fresh; it should be wrapped in a clean, dry cloth, and kept in an airy place. If you use a bin, see that it lets in air—either by air-holes or keeping the lid tilted.

4   If, in spite of your care, you sometimes get stale ends, use them up in cooking—or, as a last resort, put them in the pig-food bin. Never, *never* put them in the dustbin.

Issued by Ministry of Food   June 1946   6498106

Fig. 13. The Bread Code - signifying the post-war austerity

In preparation of this chapter, I have used standard sources for local history research, and more particularly:

Chichester City Plans (BO/CH/16/1); Electoral Registers; Chichester City Valuation List 1934 BO/CH/34/5; Chichester City Rates 1914 BO/CH/35/1; Add Mss 48,420-48,421; Add Mss 52,604-52,605; Memories of Sheila M. Clayton née Syrett; Ancestry website (Census and GRO records); GOAD Maps

2
FISH FARM AND FOREST

TERRY CARLYSLE & PAUL FOSTER

To be a vegetarian, and even more so a vegan, is to deny
the exquisite tantalus of Blood (Anon)

'Fish, farm, and forest' is one of those alliterative phrases that immediately engage attention and, once met, sit in the memory somewhat unthinkingly. In this instance the phrase – at least a similar phrase – appeared as an advertising slogan painted on the wall above a shop at 22-23 East Street: Byerley & Co. – currently, Field & Trek. As the phrase suggests, the produce for sale included everything from the three realms named – sea, farm, and forest; and that is the subject of this chapter. But before proceeding it is worth remembering that with the demise (currently) of all butchers within the city walls, there has been lost not only an awareness of seasonality but also a vivid consciousness of the role of fishermen, farmers, herdsmen, and the 'bloody' outcome of their labour.

Fig. 1. The East Street location of Byerley & Co.

Notions of seasonality are quickly made: salmon fishing, for instance, had a customary season from 11th February through to 31st October. Fish caught early in the season and even on into high summer were generally scarce and expensive, so one particular schoolboy, with whom the present writer was intimate, tasted salmon rarely, and only ever in late August or September. A similar seasonality applied to spring lamb, veal and, to change the focus, pullets – female chicken under a year old. With the arrival over the past thirty or so years of fish farms and large poultry farms, we have increasingly lost this awareness, in connexion with food, of many such natural rhythms of life – not just in the seas, but also on land. For many, that is a loss to be regretted.

Consequent upon this change has been the loss to Chichester of its cattle market. At one time, because of the hinterland of the Downs and, equally significantly, because of the

nearness of Britain's primary dockyard at Portsmouth (and the demand it generated), the market at Chichester was, after Smithfield in London, the second largest in the country. Flourishing for several centuries (but moved from the streets in 1871 to the site in Market Avenue), the closure of the Market arrived more than twenty years ago - in October 1990, and brought to an end scenes celebrated by poets and others, E. V. Lucas commenting just over 100 years ago about the number of 'tilt carts, each bringing [on market day][1] a farmer or farmer's wife' dressed in her finest, and certainly wearing a hat! Such scenes are now in memory only, but each of the businesses below are reminiscent of that past world.

Fig. 2. The cattle market in East Street (and Eastgate Square) prior to the establishment of the Cattle Market off Market Avenue in 1871

CRIPPS, MISS AGNES, The Buttermarket

The luxuriously refurbished Market House building known, erroneously,[2] as the Buttermarket no longer looks a likely home for butchers, fishmongers and grocers. It was however, from its opening back in 1808, designed to enable local traders, such as one Miss Agnes Cripps, to sell their wares; in her case as a fishmonger from the 1930s to the 1970s. Her name is widely remembered amongst those born and bred in Chichester; time and again the words 'my mother bought our fish from her' have been heard. As to why fish and why the Market House, the answers come from her sister, Miss Anne Cripps. Apparently, during the early 1930s, Agnes had helped out 'from time to time'

1   Records show that early last century up to 7,000 sheep might be sold at the market; post WW2, there was an increased focus on pigs, and a 1000 a week were often traded.

2   'But was Chichester's Market House ever a Butter Market?' Alan Green (2011) *Chichester History* No 27 pages 33-37

3   Letter from Miss Anne Cripps to the author dated 6th August 2011

Fig. 3. The interior of the Market House with fish stalls to the rear in 1939.

the 'gentleman that had the Tenancy in the Butter Market'. [3] This must have been the Peter Arnett whose name appears in the street directories for several years before 1936. At some stage, in 1935, he stopped trading and after a short while, well before the days of women's liberation, Miss Cripps 'decided to apply to the Council for the tenancy hoping she could make it work as a way of making a living'.[4] Her name then appears, under the 'Buttermarket' heading, in all the street directories for Chichester until these were discontinued in the mid 1970s.

Miss Cripps, and her fish, are even now remembered with affection. These memories generally recall her selling fish in the company of her sister and her brother James. James had also sold fish and poultry in his shop at 105 The Hornet; this shop had already been a fishmonger's (William Mason's) before he rented it from late 1936 or early 1937. The onset of war meant that James decided to close the shop (probably no later than 1940) after which he was called up into the army for 6 years. The War also affected Miss Cripps's location in the Market House as she had to move her three fish stalls in 1943, to a position near the entrance, from her previous site at the rear. This move was decided upon by Chichester's Emergency Committee in response to a request from Mr Stringer (Proprietor of Stringers, Tent Contractors), of Chapel Street.[5] Being unable to continue in his factory, after enemy action had destroyed much of that building, he sought, and gained, permission to rent the back section of the Market House as temporary accommodation.

Miss Cripps's stall always remained in the Market House, to which fish supplies mainly came from Grimsby and Hull (with kippers from Scotland). Deliveries came in the early years by sail and latterly by road when their very early morning arrival into North Street was said to be not to the liking of Mr Bastow.[6] As with so many other accounts of small businesses those involved with fish helped out one another when

4   op. cit.
5   WSRO CS/1 18/2/1943
6   Information derived from notes of a telephone conversation between Sheila Hale and Miss Anne Cripps in April 2011.

necessary so that, in the 1940s, when Mrs Long (proprietor of F. Shippam Fried Fish Shop at 77c St Pancras ran out of fish she would tell her young son, Garry, to get on his bike to go and ask 'Agnes for a stone of cod' and his trip there would not be in vain. Miss Cripps continued to run her stall with James (upon his return to civilian life) and Anne until she died in 1976 when the shop was closed.

C. J. ELPHICK, pork butcher, 71 East Street

Fig.4. Elphick's in East Street.

The pork butcher business trading under the name C. J. Elphick originates with Charles John Elphick, born in Hadlow, near Tonbridge in Kent, as long ago as 1865. Records show the shop was in business by 1901 for then CJ is recorded as working at the shop in East Street, becoming by 1911 the manager. Noted particularly for the savour of its pork sausages, an assistant who worked at the shop after WWII for thirty years, reports that although the pork meat came unboned (from Arundel), the actual seasoning arrived in large tubs from a firm in Bristol called Lucas Ingredients. Founded in 1926 and still trading, the firm specializes in food flavourings and has an international clientele. Mysteriously, Elphick's skilfully promoted the idea that the recipe was so special that it would never be revealed, and supported this by ensuring no member of the public could ever see the sausages being made – which occurred in the cellar, thus ensuring the commercial seasoning was kept well away from any prying eyes of the public!. Charles Elphick died soon after WWII, and the firm was then run until its closure in 1987 by a partnership of Mrs Hall (of the East

Fig. 5. Victor Goodeve serving at the counter, with customers queuing – such was the popularity of the business

Street grocery business, Harris & Hall - see page 50), Charlie Hawkins – manager (but later replaced by Donald Bateson), and Bertie Adams.

When the shop closed, the very last pork sausage was eaten by a local resident, Tony Poucher: he had planned to freeze it for posterity (so highly regarded was the recipe), but his wife had other ideas and cooked it!

W. GOODGER, 2 West Street/ 18 East Street/ 42 The Hornet

The Goodger family were long associated with the butcher's trade; claiming, in some of their advertisements to have been established in 1753. Such early date, however, is well before any Goodgers were recorded trading as butchers within Chichester. This particular branch of the numerous Goodger family, a name that was most frequently spelt as Goodger but also as Goodyer and Goodyear, can be traced in many West Ashling records dating from the eighteenth century onwards. Details of when exactly they became involved in the trade of butchers are not clear but by 1813 Thomas Goodyer was described as Butcher West Ashling when his daughter was baptised (and he was similarly described two and six years, later when his names was entered on the baptismal register as Goodger). Thereafter such records and the censuses

Fig. 6. 1926/27 Trade Directory

contain frequent references to members of this West Ashling branch of Goodgers who were either master or journeyman butchers.

Exactly when the family decided to expand their business to run a shop in Chichester is not clear. However, it would seem to have occurred by 1895 when a street directory entry for Chichester records William and Arthur Goodyear as butchers at 2 West Street whilst these same two brothers appear (albeit with their surname spelt Goodger), under West Ashling, as butchers and farmers. Although the Chichester shop was in their two names it seems to have been run by one of William's sons (also William) who moved to Chichester before 1898 and appeared with his wife and children on the 1901 census as butcher manager at 2 West Street. There seems to have been some indecision over the exact name of the shop, as recorded in the street directories (between William Goodger, William Goodger Junior and Goodger Brothers) but regardless of this minor confusion the business appears to have flourished so that in 1914 the shop can be seen in a photograph, at its new location of 18 East Street (a move that probably occurred during 1913), looking prosperous and well staffed.

Fig. 7. On the back of this picture appear the words Christmas Show 1914.

Trade continued here until the mid 1930s when the shop was moved, for the last time, to 42 The Hornet. By 1950 the shop, whilst still displaying the Goodger name, had as its proprietors C. and L. Cosens. An article in the *Chichester Observer* for January 17th 1985 described the then proprietor, Lawrence Cosens, who was well known in the area for the large display of local pheasants, turkeys, rabbits and venison which appeared outside his shop before Christmas. He claimed that he had never had a day's holiday from the shop since he and his father had taken it over forty years before, and stated that he prepared all the game and other meat using traditional methods only. This article referred to him having one assistant who was named in an article (of unidentified origin and date, but probably some five years later) as Mrs Angela Lee who had, by that time, worked for Mr Cosens for 28 years. The later article marked the purchase of the business by David McElwee, then of McElwee's Natural Food Warehouse in Arundel. David announced his desire to continue the notion of farm field and forest at the shop. At that date, the McElwee company were ahead of the times, believing themselves to be the first in the country to wish to sell additive free meat, asking their farmer suppliers to avoid all colouring and hormones. Sadly, the shop was not to outlast the century.

CHARLIE HOWARD, butcher, 81 North Street

Charlie Howard is one of the very few Chichester tradesmen whose names have appeared in the pages of The Times newspaper, albeit not in relation to his activities as a butcher. His local popularity and many interests and success in the sporting world rather overshadow his more trade orientated predecessor and successors. Charlie (not Charles) was born on the 27th of September 1854; the son of George and Mary Howard, from Hampshire, who moved to North Street in Chichester, where George founded a butcher's shop in the late 1850s. George, described as a master butcher in the 1861 census, was not to enjoy his shop for long as he died in 1872, leaving his relict, Mary, to take over the shop and his effects (valued at under the value of £450 according to the Probate Register).

Fig. 8. Chichester Directory J. W. Moore (1909)

According to an article extolling the virtues of Chichester, dated circa 1896, Charlie took on the responsibility for a large part of the business following his father's death but this did not stop his interest in sport in general or his cricket playing in particular.[7] Playing for Sussex from 1874 – 1882 and scoring the top average for Sussex in 1879 Charlie enjoyed such popularity that Priory Park subscribers (who paid to enjoy the delights of the park!) were happy to forego 72 hours of their rights to use the park, to allow a three day match to be played there between Lord March's XI and the Australian Team on 28th-30th June 1886 for his benefit. He was a long time member of the Priory Park Cricket Team and also acted as Captain of the local football club on occasion as well. His interests also extended to horse racing and he was to breed and race, successfully, a horse that he named Priory Park. It was the sale of Priory Parks' half sister Chichester Chimes for five thousand pounds to Lord Woolavington in 1928 that was to merit one of the several brief references to Charlie in the Times. Another, more sombre, account occurred in 1924 when, on the 3rd of March, The Times reported that Charlie (here of course referred to as Mr C Howard) had offered a reward of £25 for information leading

7 *Views and Reviews Special Edition Chichester* W T Pike & Co Publishers, Grand Parade Brighton (c1896) p25-26
8 Op. Cit.

Fig. 9. Charlie Howard's shop, with the Royal Warrant displayed above the frontage

to the arrest of the murderer of local girl Vera Hoad.

Charlie's shop was described as possessing 'that air of freshness and cleanliness which make the butcher's shop of the present such a marked contrast to its prototype of a previous generation.'[8]

Highlighting how storage requirements have altered over time the article went on to state that 'a notable feature of the establishment is a large, cool room where customers can have their meat hung in hot weather.' According to the same article business had doubled in the preceding few years and an advertisement for the shop in 1905 listed Charlie's more prominent customers, including the Bishop of Chichester, the Duke of Richmond, the Earl of March, Lord Gifford and Lady Hamilton.[9] Impressive though this list might be it was as nothing to Charlie's most illustrious customer of all, King Edward VII, marked by the 1910 award of a Royal Warrant.[10] A Royal Coat of Arms was affixed above his shop thereafter and indeed remained there till the shop closed.

Charlie is said to have sold the shop in 1928, the year preceding his death (leaving some £21,011 in effects) on 20th May 1929 in Chichester.[11] To whom did he sell the shop? A photograph of Charlie outside, his shop, along with several others may hold the answer.[12] Amongst those listed is Oswald Collins who is described as the manager. It would be quite possible that the manager might have taken over the shop. The name of the shop reverted to Charlie Howard by 1933, perhaps the cachet of the name was diminished if seen in tandem with another less well-known one. It was not until 1950 that the proprietor's name was listed and then it was an H. Cosens (which excites interest as A. and L. Cosens were proprietors of Goodger's butcher shop). The directories relate that in 1954 the proprietor was C. A. Foster and then in 1964 H. J. Burbage. Of these people there is no obvious record currently available so all that can be said is that the shop closed (according to Ken Green)in 1965. There was, for several years after that date, a butcher's shop named C. Howard at no 8 St Pancras. Councillor Anne Scicluna believes that the business from North Street moved to St. Pancras, and her mother used to get her meat there for some years. She also noted that 'there was a man named Murphy who worked there, and who became something of a friend with my

9 *The Sussex Blue Book and Court Directory* (1905)

10 *Chichester Remembered* Ken Green (1989) p20

11 op. cit.

12 *Chichester in Old Photos* Ron Harmer (1990) p48

mother and father - in later years he got them eggs every week and popped them in on Sunday mornings and had a coffee at the same time. I never knew him by any other name but Murphy. He lived in Florence Road, but died a few years ago'.

Fig. 10. Milk being delivered by tractor on 30 Dec. 1962, with Charlie Howard's shop behind

BYERLEY/HOOPER, fishmonger and poulterers, 22-23 East Street and
19 South Street

It was Alfred Byerley (1841-1909), one of the sons of a miller from Westbourne, who founded this firm at 22-23 East Street at least as far back as 1870. After the death of his first wife, Alfred married for a second time and set up home at The Retreat, Lyndhurst Road. His new wife acted as book-keeper for the firm, and his daughter, Jessie, (born 1872) took on the role of cashier.

Thomas Kimbell (1814-1872) and his wife Rosanna, moved their large family from Fencott, Oxfordshire, to the Chichester area sometime around 1856 and he set up business in George Street as a grocer. From this marriage has come Thomas Pain Kimbell, pork butcher and provision merchant in East Street (shop front at the beginning of this chapter); Francis Morris Kimbell, grocer and corn dealer; his son William, baker, confectioner & caterer, 15 East Street; his son, Laurie, baker, confectioner and caterer who had the House of Kimbell, North Street (*see* Bread and Confectionery chapter); plus the subject of this entry, Thomas Pain Kimbell II.

At the time of the marriage of Thomas Pain Kimbell II to Rosaline Byerley at St Andrew's Church, Chichester, in October 1890, he is described as a pork butcher from Worthing but by 1901 he is shown as a fishmonger's assistant in Chichester. After the death of Alfred Byerley in 1909,[13] the business in East Street passed to Thomas Pain Kimbell II but continued under Alfred's name until 1982, passing through successive generations. In 1950 the firm (still trading as Byerley's) opened a second shop at 19 South Street, the former premises of Frederick M. Barber (F. M. Barber (Fish) Ltd.) who had

---

13   There appear to be very few (if any) members of the Byerley family now living in the Chichester area, as May Alfreda Byerley, the daughter of Alfred Owen Byerley, an innkeeper at the Wheatsheaf Inn, West Street, Bognor Regis, who lived at sometime at Lyndhurst Road, was recorded at death (Nov. 1941) as being of Shifnal Cottage [1 Oldwick Meadows], Lavant.

traded on that site as a fishmonger and poulterer since 1901. With this move, Barber continued for a few years in smaller premises at 8 South Street; and the then Kimbell running Byerley's closed the East Street store about 1954.

With the onset of the Harold Macmillan years (the 'never had it so good' speech was 1957), the deprivation

Fig. 11. Thomas Pain Kimbell (d. 1933) and his son (Tom) with the shop's Christmas display for 1913

of the war years must have seemed a distant memory. At that time supplies were severely restricted and the shop was often able to sell fish only a couple of times a week; and when news that a stone of fish was expected long queues formed in East Street for several hours. Inevitably, conditions then were a far cry from those before WW II: then Byerley's employed a staff of 22, but the weekly wages bill was restricted to £21.00, which included several staff working at The Retreat in Lyndhurst Road, growing fruit, vegetables, flowers, as well as keeping pigs.

The busiest time was always Christmas: staff used to visit local farms to kill and pluck the turkeys; and there was always anxiety about the weather: with no refrigeration,

a moist, even partially warm week before Christmas turned the plucked birds green - with great loss of sales.

But despite Macmillan's claim, when the 1960s and 70s arrived, trading as an independent selling perishable foods proved increasingly difficult, as was the problem

Fig. 12. Hoopers in South Street

14 And before, as George Hooper, a well-regarded fishmonger in Southampton, was in business there in the1820s.

of finding suitable and reliable staff; and in 1984 Dick Kimbell retired, and sold the business.

Byerley's obtained most of their fish from Hoopers, a long-established (1832)[14] Portsmouth fishmonger with commercial interests as well as retail. It was not, therefore, surprising that when the last Mr. Kimbell decided to retire, Hoopers decided to buy the business. The shop was rebranded as Hooper Fresh Fish Shop and continued trading until 1998, the then proprietor, John Hooper, being the fifth generation of the Hooper family to spend a career with the beauty that swims in the sea.

J. PRIOR, Quality Butcher, Buttermarket, North Street

In October 1957, Jim Prior and a partner (who left shortly afterwards to work elsewhere) opened a butcher's shop in the Buttermarket. Although small in size, it fully justified its tag-line, 'Quality Butcher', and was much appreciated by local residents. One might have thought that most of the meat was local – but that was only partly so. It is true that the lamb and pork came from the meat market at Portsmouth (Norway Road), but the beef came from much further afield - direct from Scotland, from Aberdeen no less!

Fig. 13. Jim Prior serving a customer at his shop in the Buttermarket

Apparently, the driver left his home in Arbroath every Saturday, drove north to the market in Aberdeen and, after loading with prized Aberdeen Angus beef, began his journey south. For Saturday night he stopped in Carlisle, and then travelled on down to Smithfield - to be in London very early on Monday morning. After the necessary negotiations, he then came down to Chichester, usually delivering by midday and, after other stops at Southampton, began the long journey home, to be back in Arbroath on a Wednesday – until the week's work began again on Saturday . . . so his 'weekend' was always a Thursday and Friday!

Jim maintained the business until 1989 when, along with other shopkeepers in the Buttermarket, circumstances forced retirement. The closure marked not just the end of a valued butcher, together with similar shops - for adjacent was a greengrocer (H. White) and, at the head of the market, a fishmonger, but of a valued service that met many of the basic needs of local residents, all in a single covered market. *Tempora mutabantur* – the times were changing!

Fig. 14. Interior of Shippam's shop on South Street

SHIPPAMS, 4 South Street (earlier 48 East Street, and earlier still (1786) on Westgate)

The firm can trace its existence to 1786, which was when Charles Shippam opened a grocery shop in Westgate, but the great leap forward was achieved by Charles' grandson (also Charles, 1828-1897, who was established by 1851 at 48 East Street as a bacon curer and pork butcher) and by this Charles' son, Alfred Earnest Cooper Shippam (1874-1947). The first factory was built in 1892, and it was at this time that they began cooking meat for the famous jars – initially earthenware, glass being introduced in 1905; and soon after were supplying canned sausages to British troops fighting in South Africa. This same year (1905), Alfred and his four brothers who worked in the firm formed a partnership of equals (previously shares in the company had been allocated by age); and the following year the firm received a public accolade in the *Daily Mail* (23 June, 1906) which reported that Shippams ran 'an ideally clean and well-managed factory for providing the public with first-class foodstuffs, cleanly and carefully handled throughout all procedures and stages of preparation'. The public approbation led to a considerable increase in sales, and Scott, for instance, was to take cases of the products (including Christmas puddings) to the Antarctic on the 1910 expedition. At that time, the potted meats and pastes provided only 40% of sales, but within a year or so that percentage rose to over 70% - a staggering increase, which was accompanied by a huge development in the range of flavours – 'thirteen meat and thirteen fish pastes, as well as other products including galantine of wild boar's head and yachting pies' being recorded, all of which were produced in a new factory at East Walls dating from 1913.

Between the wars, the firm developed the family nature of the business. In 1923 Alfred Shippam had taken on the role of general manager, and in 1924 he initiated annual company outings; started a club house for employees in 1927 and the following began a profit sharing scheme, followed in 1939 by a pension scheme. Most of the staff spent their whole working lives with the firm, which never made anyone redundant and always found jobs for the children and grandchildren of employees, even if there was no need for extra labour. In 1924 the factory was honoured by a visit from Queen Mary, who was presented with a miniature paste jar filled with anchovy paste, for the royal dolls' house; and soon after the consequent publicity the firm was producing over a million jars of paste a year.

During World War II many of the workforce were called up, and women began to be employed in 1942. Alfred, the last of the original five partners still active in the business, managed the company with the help of his nephew Bassil, and in 1947 the firm was awarded a royal warrant of appointment as suppliers of meat and fish pastes to HM King George VI. Alfred himself did not live long after the end of the war, dying on 13 April 1947 at his home, 2 Cawley Road; but the firm continued under Bassil Shippam for another generation, until 1974 when the business was bought by an American company, William Underwood of Boston, and later became part of Princes Foods Manufacturing Group, now owned by Mitsubishi, but founded in 1880 at Liverpool.

Fig.15. Shippam sign c. 6.25 am, 18 August 2000 - the day of its removal

Grateful thanks for assistance with this chapter to: Anne Cripps, Victor Goodeve, Garry Long, and Anne Scicluna.

3
PROVISIONING THE KITCHEN CABINET

KEN GREEN & SHEILA HALE

Food for thought is no substitute for the real thing
(Walt Kelly)

The Grocers' Company (No. 2 in precedence of the Great Twelve City Livery Companies) was formed out of the Pepperers who dealt in spices, drugs, and tobacco, often coming from Italy and being connected with Italian merchants who had settled in London. They became responsible for inspecting and cleansing or garbling spices and also for regulating the weighing of all heavy imported goods by using the King's Beam. Ordinances were drawn up for the Pepperers in 1345 but by 1373 the company became known as Grocers or properly 'Grossers' because they dealt in bulk, i.e. were wholesale merchants. They were powerful with their first Charter in 1428 but suffered a loss in 1617 when the Apothecaries broke away, taking the drug business, and were nearly ruined when the Great Fire of 1666 destroyed the Hall and practically all the rentable property.

Fig. 1. A 1950s kitchen cabinet

Before the days of fitted kitchens (cupboards, worktops and appliances) units would be free standing and one item in particular which was highly coveted by the housewife of the 1940s and 1950s, was the kitchen cabinet. Models varied, of course, but the combinations were similar; two cupboard doors at the top (often glass – sometimes sliding), with perhaps a couple of cutlery drawers below; then a pull-down enamel or formica work surface at a suitable height for rolling-out pastry etc. and storage for jars or bags of flour, sugar, dried fruit and the like behind; below, two more doors (often with ventilation discs on them for storing vegetables and fruit, or bread). A wonderful design for a small space and considered very smart at the time, except that when preparing, say, pastry, flour often escaped through the hinge to the floor though, of course, advertisements failed to show this flaw!

GEORGE BUNN (ORCHARD FRUIT STORES), 57 East Street

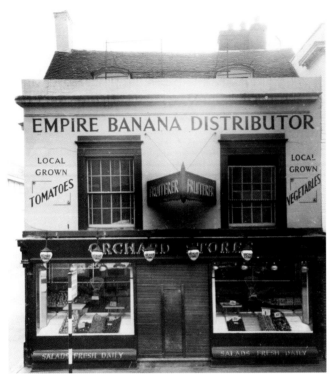

Fig. 2. Orchard Stores in East Street on the site now occupied by Caffé Nero

For those of us who can remember the War years, the Orchard Stores in East Street, popularly known as Bunn's, will always evoke memories of the queues that formed outside of the shop on the rumour of supplies of scarce fruits to be had. Not bananas, but the more available apples, pears, sometimes plums and very occasionally oranges.

Before the First World War, George Bunn had been a horse trader based in Essex, but when he was called up he served in the Veterinary Corps. On being demobbed he decided that in view of the growing effect of the motor car on the horse trade, he should look for a different future.

Coming to Chichester in 1920 with his wife, Alice, he purchased a greengrocery shop in George Street; in addition he set up a stall in Baffin's Lane selling fruit and vegetables. In c.1927 he sold the shop, which became a bakery, and moved his business to 57 East Street on the corner of Baffin's Lane, living on the first floor. As the shop thrived, George moved into the wholesale side of the trade, supplying many other local shops as well as hotels and restaurants. By now joined

Fig. 3. Orchard Stores on the corner of East Street and Baffin's Lane

by his eldest son, George Bunn junior, they became the area distributors for Empire Bananas. Arriving in a green state from the West Indies via Southampton Docks, the bananas were stored in specially adapted heated cellars below the East Street premises for ripening.

George still maintained his interest in horses and purchased a twenty acre wetland site in Selsey known as Pidney's Marsh for grazing purposes. In the mid 1950s he sold this land to his youngest son, Douglas who, having obtained permission to use it as a caravan park, had it drained and in 1959 opened it as the White Horse Caravan Park complete with a shop, office and Club House. West Sands and Green Lawns Holiday Parks followed to form the largest caravan holiday complex in Europe. Douglas Bunn went on to create the All England Jumping Course, in the grounds of his Sussex home at Hickstead.

As the family became more involved with the Selsey business the East Street shop was sold to the Portsmouth firm of H. Wain & Sons Ltd. The premises were later used by Melbray, fruiterers and Quartons, fruiterers. The site is now occupied by the Caffè Nero coffee house.

Fig. 4. Hopkins & Son

J. W. HOPKINS & SON, grocers, 36 West Street

There is now no trace of the above premises which were demolished in 1961 after 100 years of trading. The volume of traffic through Chichester had increased to such an extent that the decision was taken to remove some of the properties in Westgate which formed a narrow bottle-neck impeding the flow of cars, heavy goods vehicles and buses. Numerous other properties were pulled down including the house on North Walls once the home of Eric Gill.

James Hopkins was born in West Wittering to Charles and Martha Hopkins in 1835, one of twelve children. Charles Hopkins had a butcher's shop at 28 South Street where James grew up. He studied art, learnt to play the flute and attended Charles Spring's Grammar School at Northgate House. The 1851 Census for Chichester shows him at Northgate, apprenticed to a Master Grocer, Thomas Gadd, who had a sizeable establishment housing Mr. and Mrs. Gadd, three daughters, two visitors, one grocer's assistant, two apprentices and two servants. However, James did not complete his apprenticeship and left after two years and three weeks, the final straw, according to a letter he wrote to his sisters in 1853, occurring when he was expected to push the fully loaded hand-cart up the hill to the Barracks on his own whereas, previously, he had had the assistance of a boy. Generations of the Gadd family were grocers in Chichester and in 1899 Edward John Gadd had premises at 70 North Street.

In 1857 James Hopkins began his own grocery business at 36 West Street. The property lay back from the road, with a length of grass in front, just at the entrance to the North Walls. He married Mary Ann Elstone in 1860 and they had five children, three of whom sadly died in 1869 supposedly of diphtheria. James Hopkins himself died in 1907 but his son, John William Hopkins was already working alongside him and continued the business.

An interesting glimpse of other Chichester businesses can be found among the accounts for goods supplied to Hopkins & Son by retailers and wholesalers in the city although, unfortunately, mainly for the period 1890 – 1911 so really beyond the remit of this book!

John William Hopkins (b. 1872) had worked for Harris & Hall, a family grocer and wine and spirit merchant at 2 & 3 East Street for five years before joining the family business.

Fig. 5. Harris & Hall

He, like his father, James, who had played his flute at Goodwood House, was an accomplished flautist and gave a solo performance at the Jubilee celebrations. In 1905 he first married Mary Pitcher but she died in 1913. He stood for election to the City Council, West Ward in 1912 and again in 1919. His second marriage was to Harriet Mary Lee in 1915 and they had three daughters, Doris, Frieda and Sylvia.

It was Frieda's son, Chris Anstee, who donated the family archive that Doris had collected to Chichester District Museum (including James Hopkins' Penny-Farthing bicycle and flute). In 2004, two years before her death, Simon Kitchin of the Chichester District Museum, recorded an interview with Doris in which she describes the shop during her father's time as having a cellar the full width of the shop, with brick steps down to it. On the right-hand side of the shop was a long counter with brass scales for all the dry goods (at that time supplied loose to the grocer), and a glass case behind. On the centre back wall there were goods displayed and a second counter on the left with another set of brass scales for weighing and serving cheese, bacon, lard and butter. A chair at each counter was

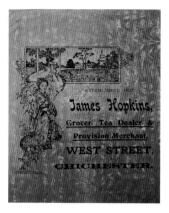

Fig. 6. *James Hopkins: a paper bag*

supplied for customers to rest whilst their orders were assembled!

With the advent of the Portsea Island Mutual Co-operative Society Ltd, grocers, in North Street in the 1930s and their offer of dividend, followed by the Second World War restrictions, it must have become a very different shop. A Ministry of Food Licence dated 1942, shows they were no longer licensed to sell bacon, ham, cheese, fish, fruit curds, game or meat. Other changes had taken place, too, for instead of being supplied with goods from other local traders, a Memo book for 1958 shows they were regularly ordering their goods, pre-packed, from Messrs Willis Holder & Lee Ltd., Brighton.

Harriet Hopkins continued to run the business during her husband's illness but closed it down after his death at their home at 8 North Walls in 1958. 36 West Street was sold to West Sussex County Council for their road-widening scheme and demolished in 1961.

MICKEY'S, general provisions and confectionery, 47 North Street

For many older Cicestrians just the mention of Mickey's shop in North Street will bring a smile to their face, and most will have a story to tell about him - some unrepeatable. Mickey was more than a shopkeeper, he was an institution: few, however, knew of his generosity to local hospitals. Mickey's father, Emidio Guarnaccio, immigrated to England from Italy in 1907. After several jobs, he returned home to marry his fiancée, Petromilla, and bring her back to this country where they became landlords of a public house in Petersfield, later moving to the 'Old House at Home' at Havant.

In 1920, now with three sons, Michael, Peter and John, they purchased a grocery and general stores in Northgate, Chichester, with lodging rooms behind the premises. They became well known for the Ice Cream that they made and sold, Emidio and his sons pushing their 'Stop

Fig. 7. *Mickey and his shop*

Me and Buy One' wheelbarrow around the City's streets and parks, and to the beach at Selsey.

They sold their business in 1929 when they moved to a newly-built house in Whyke Road which included an annexe for them to continue manufacturing their ice cream. In 1933, Mickey purchased premises at 47 North Street, which at one time had been the Foresters Arms pub, and set up his own general stores. Every day, including Sundays, he opened the shop before seven o'clock each morning, closing at ten in the evening, Mickey would always have a cigarette in his mouth, using a scale weight as his ashtray; invariably he wore a waistcoat and a cloth cap. He often gave credit to the nurses at the local hospitals. A record of their purchases, mostly for sweets and cigarettes, was chalked up on a slate behind the counter against settling day when they received their monthly cheques. This counter was originally the bar in the Foresters Arms.

During the War years Emidio, then in his mid-seventies, took over the shop while Mickey was on military service. Mickey died in 1983 and his shop was sold - initially to become a greengrocery, but nowadays it is the Orchard Tearooms.

JAMES PRIOR - GREENGROCER, 1 North House, North Street

One of the greatest pleasures as a child was to go to the local greengrocers and children in Chichester from 1959 to 1989 could indulge this delight at Jim Prior's shop in North Street – situated where the Coln Gallery is now located. The delight was mainly to do with the rich, vibrant colours of the fruit and vegetables, with the enormous variety of shapes and forms, and with the meticulously arranged pyramidal

Fig. 8. James Prior's greengrocery shop

displays – all within quite a confined space: in comparison, the strictly linear displays now deployed at supermarkets, with apples, say, just thrown together higgledy-piggledy in a box (with some often badly bruised) are wholly unappealing; and, of course, the supermarket has no front-of-shop, pavement display to tempt the buyers forward!

Actually, Jim and his then business partner, Roy Parker, started in 1957 with a butchery business in the Buttermarket, but when another butcher's became available at I

Fig. 9. Stephen Prior in the newly-designed interior

North House, they seized the opportunity, purchased the lease and converted it into what became a highly respected greengrocers. Early in the 1960s, Jim bought his partner out and employed a sequence of managers, several of whom, once trained by Jim, left to run their own greengrocery – in competition! Faced with this, the then partners (primarily Stephen Prior, Jim's son, and his mother, Mary) decided with the then manager, Julius Semerdak, to 'move with the times' and upgrade the shop. The 'upgrade', mainly a matter of facilitating customer self-service, was achieved by engaging Beanstalk to fit out the shop anew, a procedure that was effected in a single day, Monday 20 May 1985.

Customers welcomed the change: the turnover on many weekdays began to equal that of a Saturday, and everyone began to grapple with a new vocabulary – three-tier wall bays, inside corners, gondolas, bag rails, [shelf] barkers, flow trays, bag dispensers, and much, much more! Note above, for instance, the attractive banana rail and hooks in the new display.

Despite these popular changes, the pressure from the large supermarkets, especially in terms of cost and convenience (with parking adjacent to these new large stores, making the carrying of heavy bags considerably easier), together with a dramatic increase in annual rent – from c. £7,000 to a proposed £25,000 – led the Priors to call it a day. It was a loss to the City Centre and its residents that was keenly felt and led to a front-page feature article in the local paper (see *Chichester Observer*, 8 June, 1989). In the same paper, the same issue, in a high-lighted, boxed letter, Pamela Lander of North Close,

Fig. 10. The imposing premises on the corner of East Walls and the beginning of Eastgate Square

Chichester, wrote to deplore the loss from the City Centre of small, independent businesses: the letter, as an example of concern for a process that is now almost complete, is of historic interest – but that was of small comfort to the Priors.

SHARP GARLAND LTD, grocers and wine merchants, 1 Eastgate Square

This site had been in continuous use as a grocers shop since 1665 and was reputed to be the oldest grocery business in the country at the time of its demolition in 1964. It is said to have been founded by one, John Smith. The Hardham family ran the business for a number of years with John Hardham noted as being there in 1780; succeeded on his death in 1813 by his son, William, who died in 1833; followed by Henry John Hardham, who sold the business to Sharp Garland in 1860. The shop remained throughout wonderfully old-fashioned in appearance and the customer

Fig. 11. Raymond Duthy, *Sharp Garland interior, showing chairs for clients – a rare provision today*

service was second to none. Arched wooden fitments above drawers on the wall behind the counter housed early 19th century tea canisters; above, there was a long open shelf for jars and bottles, in front   was a row of pegs which had been used for hanging pairs of dipped rushes.

   Customers were always courteously addressed as 'Madam' or 'Sir' by the white-aproned staff and invited to sit whilst their orders were fulfilled from the hessian sacks, tins or boxes, stored behind the counter.

   Dried fruit, sugar, dried beans, peas and lentils were always weighed into thick blue paper bags, whilst greaseproof paper was the wrapping of choice for butter, cheese, and bacon, which was then placed in white bags – not a plastic bag in sight. A row of glass topped biscuit tins lined the front of the counter making selection easy for

Fig. 12. Staff at Sharp Garland from left: Charles William (Bill) Toop, Alfred Peat, Mr Aylmore, Tom Green (delivery man)

waiting customers, and the presence of cheese, bacon and roasting coffee beans filled the shop with an amazing aroma.

The Garland family were aware of their civic duties and served Chichester well. Sharp Garland was Mayor of the St. Pancras Corporation in 1871 and 1909, and the Mayor of Chichester in 1878 and 1898. His son, Sharp Archibald Garland, held the position of Mayor from 1912 to 1917; he held the same position in 1918 but by this time he was listed as Sir Sharp Archibald Garland, Kt. He was awarded the Honorary Freedom of the City in 1920.

The family home was at 'Ivybank', 10 St. John's Street. In 1924 Lady E. Garland was listed as running the YMCA in Chichester. It was their daughter, Cora, who inherited the business and when she died in 1957, she willed it to her loyal friends Vic and Eva Kent who lived nearby in St. Pancras. Mr. Alfred Peat had started with the firm as an apprentice and remained with them for nearly 60 years. Although already aged 72 when Cora Garland died, he continued to manage the business for Mr. and Mrs. Kent. He was a remarkable man in his own right, for he was an antiquarian greatly interested in Sussex church heraldry and he also had an encyclopaedic knowledge of furniture, pottery and porcelain.

The City Council made a compulsory purchase order on the building with the intention of widening the road; this was never done and at some stage the building was deemed to be unsafe. In 1964, just short of the 300th anniversary of the founding

of the shop, it was demolished, and the site sold to a developer (Sharp Garland House and Bazaar now occupy the site).

ERNEST EDWARD VOKE, fruiterer, 72 North Street

The first premises occupied by this family's fruiterers business (listed in the 1920 Directory) was at 77 North Street, then known as Voke & Son. It remained on this site for over seven years before moving to premises on the corner of Lion Street (still on the east side of North Street) where they remained for a further thirty or so years.

The Voke family were best known in Chichester as bakers as related by Frances Lansley in her chapter 'Bread & Confectionery'. They were landowners and one brother had a poultry farm at Kingsham.

Fig.13. Voke's attractive shop front in North Street

VICTOR WESTON (CITY FRUIT STORES), 21 South Street

In 1910 the residents of Chichester received a leaflet advertising the opening of a new 'High-Class Fruiterers' at 21 South Street. The shop, in premises leased from the Cathedral authorities by Mr Victor Weston, soon built up a reputation for the quality

of its produce. After the First World War Victor was joined by his two sons Cyril and Lionel and the business became known as V. C. Weston and Sons.

Cyril's son, Jim Weston, joined the business in 1958 and recalls his grandfather as being a perfectionist who would only ever accept top class produce. One of his earliest tasks was building

Fig. 14. Jim Weston's Aunt Gladys, a shop boy, Victor Weston, and Victor's mother, taken in 1920 the pyramids of apples, pears, oranges, and other fruit. that would form the display in the front window. At the rear of the shop, behind a high wall backing on to the Vicars' Close, was a small yard with an outside toilet that, Jim records, would never meet today's Health and Safety standards. In the basement, reached by steep wooden steps, there was a cold storage unit. The shop was one of the first establishments to install a deep freeze unit for the sale of frozen goods.

When Victor died in 1961, his sons continued to run the business for another 14 years but, faced with competition from supermarkets and rising rents, the shop was sold in 1975. The premises continued to be used as a greengrocery for a few years, later becoming a telephone shop and later a clothes shop.

Cyril Weston died in 1990 and Lionel in 1995. I am indebted to Jim Weston for sharing his reminiscences and knowledge of the City Fruit Stores' sixty-five years as a Chichester business.

Fig. 15. Weston's decorated for the 1953 coronation.

4
LEATHER AND LAST

Paddy Welsh

*Shoemaking: employment of 'sedentary labour [that] while it keeps the
hands fully engaged, gives little or no exercise to the mental faculties'.* Charles Crocker

In the days when boots and shoes were made with leather, and repaired with leather, it was expected that they would be worn for a while and then handed in to a shoe repairer for a new sole and maybe a new heel as well. This process was repeated several times until the time came to throw them away, or perhaps use them for gardening, and buy a new pair. Now shoes are made of something else and the snobs and cobblers* of the past have all but vanished - some without trace, although a few are still remembered and have relatives who continue as part of Chichester.

As with many things in the modern world, change crept up on us and soon we were part of a society that had little use for traditional leather soles and heels and, certainly, became less and less familiar with working people's boots. Astonishingly, in the early decades of last century, Chichester (as listed in Kelly's 1911 Chichester Directory) possessed all of thirty-two boot makers. In contrast, after World War Two there were but a dozen or so boot and shoe repairers in the city, although most of them were still cheery establishments where you had a chat with the repairer and arranged to call back in a few days.

Historically, the most famous of Chichester's shoemakers was Charles Crocker (1797-1861), reputed to be also half-saint and half-poet. Although he is not strictly included in our look at more modern cobblers, he merits inclusion because he established the pedigree of the profession locally. Educated at the Grey Coat School in Chichester for four years – until he was 11, Crocker then spent seven years in apprenticeship. For forty years after that, he worked on his own in Little London, combining shoe repairing with writing poems and sonnets, many of them published. He wrote to his publisher: 'I started early in life with a determination to write verse as well as my unassisted mental powers would allow. At the commencement of my literary career I formed a resolution to which I have through life adhered, and that was never to write a line calculated to wound the feelings, injure the reputation or contaminate the morals of any human being'.

---

* ['Cobbler' is a very old, even mediaeval, term for a shoemaker and, as now, implied rather poor workmanship; 'snob', originally a nickname for a shoemaker, is a much more recent usage, the first record being dated 1785 – thirty years after Johnson's *Dictionary* (1755). *Eds*]

From 1845 Crocker was appointed Sexton to the cathedral, and later bishop's verger. It is said the fall of the cathedral spire in 1861 was such a shock to him that he died seven months later! The previous year (1860), a complete edition of his poems had been published by Mason and Wilmshurst of Chichester, a firm that had employed Crocker in its book department for part of the last decade of his life. Much earlier, Mason published Crocker's, *The Vale of Obscurity, the Lavant, and Other Poems* (1830).

CHARLES RILEY, 26 Caledonian Road

Charles Riley, one of 14 children, was born at 26 Caledonian Road and carried on business at the shop attached to it. He was born with a deformity and had a humped back, but it affected neither his work nor his sense of fun, for he had a parrot in his shop, which talked to him and the customers. There was a constant stream of children calling at the shop to have a word with Polly, and she is remembered as having a word or two for everyone.

Relatives cannot remember how long he was in business at Caledonian Road, but it was for 'years and years - all his working life'. He worked first with his father, also a shoe repairer, and eventually took over the business. He died at Caledonian Road in 1969.

Fig.1. Charles Riley and parrot

H.J. PETTO AND SON, 16 Northgate

The name Petto dominated the Chichester shoe-repairing scene for 75 years. Henry Albert James Petto was born in 1921 at the shop in rented premises on Northgate with the words Petto and Son on the sign outside. He worked with his father, also Henry, just as his father had worked with his father – another Henry – in the years before. The three of them served the city for 75 years, the first Henry starting the business in Whyke Lane before moving to Northgate. Henry Albert James Petto, always known as Harry, retired when he was 75 in 1996. He died aged 87.

Fig.2. Audrey and Harry Petto

Mr Petto was born above the shop, and the family recall that his mother became very ill immediately afterwards, so straw and hay were spread on the road outside to make the metal-shod wheels of carts and wagons outside less noisy. Later in his working life he and his wife, Audrey, moved to Willowbed Avenue. They had one child, a daughter, now Mrs Pamela Fisher, who lives at Tangmere.

It was Mr Petto's practice to rise early in the morning and be in the Northgate shop by seven o'clock, getting the orders ready for the day. His wife would walk their daughter to school in Chichester, and then join her husband at Northgate where she attended to the customers during the day. Mrs Fisher recalls that when her father was mending

Fig. 3. Petto and Son premises at Northgate

boots and shoes, he would put the nails in his mouth and take them out one by one as he needed them (a practice adopted by many shoe repairers). She remembers that when he was old and retired he had all his own teeth, although the front ones were worn down by the nails.

Mr Petto's working day was long. He went home to Willowbed Avenue for a meal in the evening, but would then return to the Northgate premises to get on with the next day's work. His great relaxation was playing the piano, and he kept it going long into retirement even though his hands had become arthritic. Mr Petto's only time away from the business was during World War Two when he joined the army and served in Italy.

Fig. 4. Noyce's shop in The Hornet

HAROLD G. NOYCE, 124 The Hornet

Harold G. Noyce left school in 1917 aged 12 and went to work with his father, George, at 124 The Hornet, eventually taking over the business. He worked at the same premises until his late 60s or early 70s. The shop was too small to be the family home and he lived variously at Bognor Road, Ormonde Avenue, and Whyke Lane. He married a girl from the New Forest and they had three children. Mr Noyce could make shoes and boots as well as repair them, but he was not enthusiastic about that side of the business, probably because it was a long hard process making shoes and boots. Repairing was much simpler and probably there was more money in it! He died in 1986.

WILFRED LEVER, 12 Adelaide Road

Wilfred Lever ran his repair business for 40 years at this address. After leaving school at 12, he was apprenticed to Charlie Hennings at 71 North Street, Chichester, and at the end of that time started on his own at Adelaide Road, some time in the 1930s. He and his wife had a family of two girls and one son, all still living in Chichester. He died just over 30 years ago.

C.A. HENNINGS, 71 North Street

Charlie Hennings ran his bootmaking business for many years in North Street, at a shop next but one to the corner of Lion Street. The ground floor and cellars were used for his business and the family – his wife and two children – lived above. His daughter, Mrs Joan Young recalled her happy childhood at the shop in an interview some years ago. She said: 'I loved the smell of leather, and the noise of the machines down in the cellars. When a large machine was in use, the whole house seemed to shake.' Apart from being a competent worker, Mr Hennings used to sing at social gatherings in the city, and Teddy Game, the master baker who baked bread in his wood-burning oven at Broyle Road, would play the piano for him. Mr Hennings was also an able musician who played the violin and banjo; he liked a pint of beer of an evening in the Hole in the Wall in St Martin's Street.

Fig. 5. Charlie Hennings' premises

H.G. FERRY (ERBAN KAZIMIERZ), 21 The Hornet

Fig. 6. The Ferry-Kazimierz shop frontage

A well-loved member of the shoe-repairing fraternity in Chichester was Polish-born, Erban Kazimierz. He was the son-in-law of another well-known shoemaker Mr H. G. Ferry, with whom he worked for many years, and took over the business at The Hornet on Mr Ferry's death in 1960.

Mr Kazimierz married Mr Ferry's daughter Doris at Stanmore, Middlesex, in 1947, and then moved to Chichester to help Mr Ferry with the business. He was a pleasant individual, always ready for a cheery chat with his customers, especially about the Third Programme classical music that played most of the time in the background. He entered into the spirit of the thing when the customer guessed at the name of the piece being played, and said, 'Nearly!' when the customer got it wrong.

Born in Sanok in southern Poland near the Russian border, he came to England after fighting with the Polish army against the German and Russian invaders. He spent the rest of the war in Scotland and southern England, and was involved in anti-invasion and other work, about which he said very little. He kept in touch with three sisters in Poland, and sent them food parcels when times were particularly hard. He never returned to his homeland, and would answer questions about it with the dry remark: 'l had lots of long-term plans before the war, but unfortunately so did Hitler and Stalin.'

E. TYLER & SONS, 3a Market Avenue

If you had been browsing through the *Chichester Observer* on a day in March 1952 you would have found several advertisements assuring you that your boots and shoes would get high-class attention from local tradesmen. Under the sign of the Silver Circle was the assurance that if you took your shoe repairs to an establishment bearing the sign, *'You are dealing with a man who is pledged to supply a craftsmen's job and good materials at a fair price.'* The repairers listed were H. Petto and Son, 16 Northgate; G. Reed, 52 St Pancras; H. Smithers, Westgate; and E. Tyler and Sons, 3a Market Avenue.

Mr Tyler had another advertisement on another page stating: *'Are you looking for a square of English bend leather, a hammer, rivets, etc., - We Have Them.'* He described himself as a Leather and Grindery Merchant, and added that he ran 'the little shop with the large stock'.

D. COMBES, 51 The Hornet

Denis Combes started as a corn merchant in the 1920s at 51 The Hornet, where his father ran a hay and straw business, and around 1944 or 1945 added the Habin's Yard business of harness maker and saddler. His son, Pat Combes, joined him in the corn merchant business, taking time off when he was twenty to go to university. On his return he rejoined his father, who continued until 1968, when he retired.

As farmers gave up horses and bought tractors, the harness and saddlery business declined. In the 1950s Mr Combes, senior, added leatherwork to the business, taking on staff and installing machinery to make leather bags, cases and things of that sort. In 1974/5 the new road between The Hornet and St Pancras was made, taking a large part of the Combes property. Pat Combes continued trading as a corn merchant and supplier of pet foods and garden supplies until he retired in the late 1990s.

Mr Combes, who still lives in the city, has played a prominent part in its life for many years, and continues to do so. He was Mayor in 1975/6, and a member of Chichester District Council. He was chairman of the Fernleigh management committee which ran the well-loved city facility until the building was sold recently, and also a founder member of the Chichester and District Local History Society. He is on the management committee of a local housing association which has flats in a couple of parts of the city.

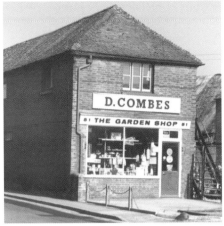

Fig. 7. The Combes shop prior to later development

RUSSELL HILLSDON, 46 South Street

Russell Hillsdon's South Street shop was known as the *Sports Store of the South*, and so it proved with many local sportsmen buying their equipment there. When

Fig. 8. The new and imposing shop on the east side of South Street

Dunlop racquets were the hottest thing in tennis and squash, they quickly appeared at Hillsdon's and everything bought there was taken back for repair and maintenance as necessary. It was a shop with a reputation and always appealed to sportsmen and women.

Russell Hillsdon started in the sports business at Barnham Market in the 1920s and then opened a shop on the west side of South Street. He moved to the other side of the road and all departments that had been at the other South Street shop were expanded. This included the gun department, which was very well supported in its day, and is still fondly remembered now. Russell Hillsdon guns are today changing hands for very large sums.

Despite the fact that he was a successful Chichester businessman, Mr Hillsdon was a loud critic of the planning rules and regulations, complaining that he had had to accept a new store which was nothing like the one he wanted. This was in the 1950s when the planners were insisting that any new building in Chichester had to have a pseudo-Georgian appearance. Mr Hillsdon wanted a bright new modern building but realized he was getting nowhere with his objections and accepted what he was allowed. Despite his objections, his shop always seemed busy and thriving. He retired in 1964 after more than half a century in the business.

HENRY TURNER & SON, 85 North Street

The shop of Henry (often known as Harry) Turner and Son was at 85 North Street for many years. Mr Turner ran these premises for the sale of good-quality footwear (agents for K shoes and Gold Cross shoes, among others). He lived in the city, in Franklin Place, and took an interest in local affairs, being President of the City Club in 1952. As was his way in those days, he sent out his bills every three months. It was said that if payers were slow, he would make a mistake in the addition and add a pound, which would bring customers rushing in to point out the error. He would apologize, amend the bill, and ask for faster payment. Those who knew him said it never failed!

Mr Turner, senior, had a boot and shoe repair business attached to his house in Franklin Place, and there for 44 years Ernest Barnes did his repairs. Mr Barnes was unusual in being deaf and dumb; when the full extent of his disability was realized, he was sent to a special school in Kent, where one of the things he learned was shoe repairing. Turner's was his only employer. Mr Barnes' daughter is Mrs Pat Samways who lives at Little Breach.

On the death of Mr Turner, senior, his son ran the business and on his death his wife continued the connection. At the end of that time it was sold, the premises now being occupied by Jones, the Bootmaker.

S.J. LINKINS, 22 and 19a South Street

Sidney J. Linkins bought the property at 22 South Street (now chesca) in 1920; it was an existing, and, evidently, very successful saddlery and harness-maker as the original lease was granted to a Mr. Miller in 1760, an apprentice (William Gambling) later taking over; subsequently, William Gambling passed the business on to his son, Robert, who had served for a period as a Corporal Saddler in the Zulu War – which included the famous Battle of Rorke's Drift (1879).

With the gradual advent of the motor car in the 1920s and 1930s, Mr. Linkins began to expand the range of work into sports equipment

Fig. 9. Linkins' shop showing a comprehensively-stocked window display

and luggage and during the war years completed orders for general leather goods, including items for the military. In 1960, Ernest H. Middleton was appointed Managing Director and quickly expanded the business to 19a South Street (now Mr. Simms Olde Sweet Shoppe), which concentrated on luggage and handbags.

For over twenty years Sidney Linkins, and his wife, Kathleen, had a house, 'Denmeads' (no. 17) on the south side of Fishbourne Road, before moving back to Worthing at the end of the 1950s. Today their former home backs onto the supermarket. As well as the two businesses devoted to leather, the record for the early 1950s also includes a confectioner, Sidney J. Linkins at 29 East Street. He was a member of Chichester Rotary Club and on his death left a legacy for the benefit of poor or deprived persons, to be run by four trustees of the Club. His death was in 1987 but the Rotary Club continues to run the charity. His wife died a few years later and the Chichester businesses vanished.

During Mr. Linkins' lifetime his business specialized in tennis racquets and sold trunks, bags, saddlery, and fancy leather goods. Repairs were done on the premises 'by experienced workmen', and an advertisement in the *Chichester Observer* on 31st December 1975 comments that the premises had been altered and extended to accommodate the complete business that 'flourishes today'.

PERCY H. SEWARD, 35 The Hornet

Seward's saddlery and harness making business had its origins in Petersfield. It was carried out there and elsewhere in Hampshire from the middle of the nineteenth century, and arrived at 35, The Hornet, Chichester, early in the 1900s, and there it stayed until it closed in 1985. Mr John

Seward, a builder of Church Lane, Eastergate, recalls that his father, Peter Seward, and his grandfather, great grandfather, and great, great grandfather were all involved in the business. He himself had a short involvement in his youth, but because of the financial climate went into building instead.

He recalls that in the early years one of the firm's biggest customers was Chichester Dairies, who had a large number

Fig. 10. Percy Seward and Jim, an employee

of horses. But the writing was on the wall when tractors started replacing horses, and the harness and saddlery business declined. One unusual customer was Douglas Bader who visited the firm and sat on a stool for an hour-and-a-half while the leather straps on his artificial legs were renewed!

In the last few years the business went over to providing fishing tackle and riding boots. It ended in 1985 with the death of Mr Peter Seward.

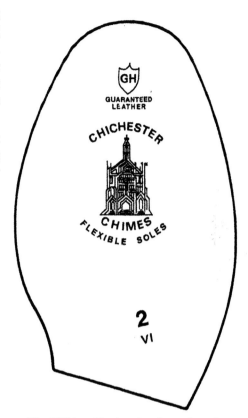

Fig. 11. A Gibbings, Harrison flexible sole, with imprint of City Cross.

The Gibbings Harrison imprint or footprint

* * *

In conclusion it's worth noting that tanning had been carried out in Chichester since medieval times, probably for at least the last 500 years.* It was centered in Westgate, where the River Lavant no doubt carried away the water, turned foul by the tanning process. Alan Green, in his *The Building of Georgian Chichester* (2007), also places a large brewery near the tannery in Westgate 'neither of which would have been entirely welcomed by residents'. Over the years the brewery was a better-known feature of Chichester, surviving until 1955 when production of Henty and Constable ale finally dried up. With an industry lasting for so many years as tanning, the buildings it occupied would have changed constantly, but there was nothing very old about The Tannery building which the County Council took over in the 1950s. It was the last of a long line of tannery buildings put up in the 1900s.

---

* There is a record that about 1550 there were 120 tanning pits in the ground, each measuring two cubic metres, 6ft wide and 6ft deep

I was aware there was a Chichester Tannery long before I even knew where Chichester was! My father was a shoemaker in a Northern Ireland village and in the 1940s got boot repairing leather from a Belfast merchant who in turn got it from England. It was sent by train and I often went to the railway station to bring home a bend (half the tanned hide of a cow). I carried it home and recall it weighed about 15lbs.

In those days leather, like everything else, was in short supply and you couldn't have what you wanted. You had to take what you were allocated or go without. My father was always very pleased when he learned he was getting a bend of Chichester leather. He liked the quality and would have had it regularly had he had the choice. I believe it was made by Gibbings, Harrison & Co. Ltd, and I seem to remember there was a tiny symbol of a circle of oak leaves printed on each bend. In mid-last century, the firm used each day a ton of oak bark (mostly from Goodwood and Cowdray) to produce up to 500 hides a week – in stark contrast to centuries ago when certain hides, known as 'Chichester Bloomed Butt' might take as long as a year to 'tan'. For further comment, see Bernard Price, Sussex People, Places, Things (1975), who claims tanning was Chichester's oldest industry. [The earliest reference to the tannery in the parish of St Bartholomew (outside Westgate, Chichester) in documents at West Sussex Record Office is dated 1703. Eds]

Other shoemakers

There were a large number of boot and shoe repairers and makers in 1950. Apart from those already mentioned were: Central Boot Co (Miss K. M. Scruse), 11 East Street; Fords (H. and S. Ford), 33 East Street; G. and W. Morton, 37 East Street; Dutton and Thorowgood Ltd, 88 East Street; John Robinson, 10 The Hornet; Henry Turner and Son Ltd, 1 New Park Road; Leonard Arthur Shier, 9a Northgate; Frederick Slaney, 12a St Martins Square; George Herbert Reed, 52a St Pancras; Bishop Brothers, 69 South Street; Harold Edward Lee, 105 Victoria Road; G. W. Smithers, 4 Westgate; Ernest Robinson, 23 York Road; but about 25 years later all that remained were: Ferry (Kazimierz), Lever, Petto, Riley, and Smithers of those already described above, and two relative newcomers: Paul's Shoe Repairs, St Martins Street, and Modern Shoe Repairs, 33 East Street.

CODA

It is worth noting that one of the London livery companies is The Worshipful Company of Loriners, a loriner being someone who makes all the metal items that are attached to harness-leather – bits, bridles, spurs, stirrups, and saddle trees – although the frame for these today uses laminated wood, notably Scandinavian birch plywood. The Company was incorporated as long ago as 1261 and is currently celebrating its 750th anniversary, but did not receive a Royal Charter until 1711, whereas the saddlers, with whom there were often disputes, received their Royal Charter in 1361.* The most important local link with the craft is the collection of William Albery (1864-1950), the former Horsham saddler who assembled in the 1920s and 1930s more than 2,000 examples of lorinery and bequeathed it to his local museum and art gallery. The collection is one of the finest in the country.

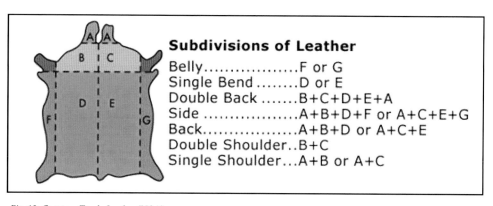

Fig. 12. Courtesy Tandy Leather (USA)

* In terms of precedence the Saddlers are listed as the twenty-sixth London Livery Company, the Loriners as the fifty-seventh.

5
LIQUID REFRESHMENT

DIANA & JIM PAYNE

I within did flow
With seas of life, like wine
(Thomas Traherne)

The government of the world [is framed] like that of Britain
in after-dinner conversations over the wine
(Henry Thoreau)

The term 'liquid refreshment' is something of a catch-all and suggests a wide range of possibilities – from, on an alcoholic spectrum, crystal clear spring water at one end to, at the other, one or other form of poteen or moonshine.[1] On a quite different kind of measure, liquid refreshment is a 'nice cup of tea', a Coke or Pepsi or, perhaps, sitting on a poolside in Hawaii – a cool beer to hand and the warm sea caressing feet dangling in the water. Such possibilities, attractive as they are, do not feature in this chapter: in contrast, the intention is to focus on what has been one of Chichester's most celebrated businesses – Arthur Purchase & Son, Wine Merchants, most recently of 31 North Street (a site now shared by Amelie and Friends, and by Strutt & Parker), but with a history stretching back into the eighteenth century.

Fig. 1. Charlotte and Stefan – baristas at Amelie and Friends

ARTHUR PURCHASE & SON, 31 North Street (formerly 65 North Street)

Records about the firm claim that its foundation can be traced back to 1780, with a continuous history through the generations of the same family until its closure after more than 200 years - which would make it one of the most enduring private retail businesses not only in Chichester, but also in the entire country.[2]

1 Typically, triple or quadruple distilled to, say, 180 proof (i.e. 90% ABV- alcohol by volume)

2 The claim of foundation in 1780 rests on oral tradition: documentary evidence suggests the business *as wine merchants* should be seen as beginning in later Victorian years (perhaps 1870, not 1780)

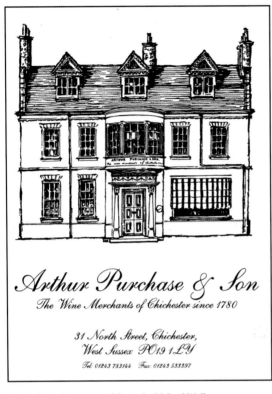

Arthur Purchase & Son

The Wine Merchants of Chichester since 1780

31 North Street, Chichester,
West Sussex PO19 1LY
Tel. 01243 783144   Fax: 01243 533397

Fig. 2. Advertising material drawn by McLeod Wallace

The earliest documentary data about the origins of the family can be traced back to a James Purchase (b. 1689) who was a Yeoman farmer in Dorset at Bere Regis, but the clearest link with a trade in alcohol begins with a Stephen Purchase, who was born in 1789, and who, in his early twenties in 1813, is shown as Innkeeper at the Egremont Arms in Chichester's South Street.[3] Later, his son, Thomas (b. 1816), is recorded as the first landlord at the Globe, Southgate, and it is evident that this interest and competence in what, today, is often referred to as the hospitality trade descended to Thomas's son, Arthur (b.1851, m. 1873 Florence Etherington of Petersfield, d.1911), who appears in the 1881 Census as the Hotel Keeper at the Globe Inn, employing four women and three men. It is evident that it was Arthur who begun the retail wine business for the 1891 Census lists him as a Wine & Spirit Merchant at Southgate; by the end of the century, however, a significant development had occurred, for Arthur moved to the North House Hotel at 67 North Street where there was a small ballroom – which must have made it an important social venue attracting a different class of clientele, as well as a large garden that ran through to St Martin's Square.

About this time, Arthur passed the management of the hotel to his daughter, Hilda Purchase, b. 1886, and pursued at 65 North Street the wine business that many Cicestrians came to know so well later in the century. Interestingly, the Visitor Book for the North House Hotel up to 1935 is still extant – at West Sussex Record Office, and the 1913 census shows that Hilda herself lived at Burton House, 66 North Street. This meant that the extended Purchase family actually occupied four closely-related properties (but not 68 North Street which was occupied by a dentist) - 65 (The Old Cross, where the wine business, A. Purchase & Son, was located), 66 Burton House

---

[3] In the 1851 census Stephen is shown as running a business in coal, and also holding office as Collector of Dues at the Canal Basin – where the charge at he Basin for a 'tun' of wine (252 gallons) was four pence, whereas the charge for a single pair of tombstones was two pence, as was an entire boat of oysters.

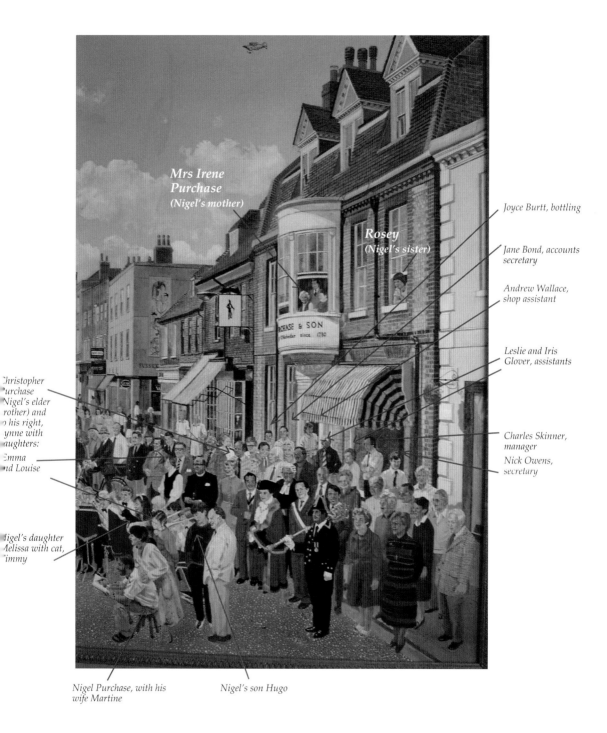

Mrs Irene
Purchase
(Nigel's mother)

Rosey
(Nigel's sister)

Joyce Burtt, bottling

Jane Bond, accounts
secretary

Andrew Wallace,
shop assistant

Leslie and Iris
Glover, assistants

Christopher
Purchase
(Nigel's elder
brother) and
to his right,
Lynne with
daughters:
Emma
and Louise

Charles Skinner,
manager

Nick Owens,
secretary

Nigel's daughter
Melissa with cat,
Timmy

Nigel Purchase, with his
wife Martine

Nigel's son Hugo

Fig. 3. Nigel Purchase, **North Street** (1985 – detail showing family and staff) – painted to commemorate
the 25th anniversary of the twinning of Chichester and Chartres, 1959-84

Fig. 4. George Arthur Russell Purchase – with his wife – in mayoral robes and insignia

(where Hilda lived), 67 North House Hotel, and 69 North Street, where another Purchase (Thomas George, b. 1874, a son of Arthur] lived with his wife, Mary – née Russell.[4] This marriage (in 1910) brought a significant new professional skill within the orbit of the wider Purchase family, for Mary (b. 1877, was the granddaughter of James Russell (b. 1809), founder in 1853 of what became a very successful photographic business in Chichester, operating from 1862-1903 out of 65 East Street as James Russell & Sons.[5]

Successful as the commercial business was, there was also issue – the Purchase whom many older Cicestrians will remember, George Arthur Russell Purchase, who was born 1913, and who became a distinguished (twice) Mayor of Chichester 1951-53; but that honour was in the future. Records show that c. 1920 his father, Thomas George, had to make hasty arrangements as the freehold at 65 North Street, owned by Ind Coope, was sold without his knowledge (or he would presumably have purchased it), and he was given short notice to leave. Fortunately, he was able to obtain premises almost opposite, at 32 North Street (now Laura Ashley, but then occupied by a Dr Ewart and used as a baby clinic), and traded there very successfully until 1956 when Russell moved the firm next door to Number 31, the fine bow-windowed property that all Cicestrians particularly associate with Arthur Purchase & Co.

This property not only holds a dramatic street position for trade purposes, but also possessed a range of outbuildings and stables at the rear, as well as a fine cellar – but

---

[4] Other members of the family, however, still plied their trade south of the Market Cross: at 57 South Street, Mary Purchase was a Lodging House Keeper and her son, Albert, an apprentice upholsterer; and Richard Purchase (son of Stephen Purchase) with his wife, Ellen, and six children, employed four men at 1 Stockbridge Road, where he continued his father's business as a Coal Merchant, and was also Collector of Dues at Chichester Canal Basin, 7,000 tons of cargo (mostly coal for the gasworks) being recorded in 1868

[5] In 1862 James exhibited at an International Exhibition held in South Kensington, a series of views of the ruins of Chichester Cathedral consequent upon the collapse, the preceding year, of the entire cathedral spire: see Chichester Cathedral Spire: the Collapse (1861), Otter Memorial Paper Number 13 (2001). The publicity gained by this led to many distinguished clients; and it may not be too fanciful to suggest that it was this same acuity of vision that later was to be practised by the artist, Nigel Purchase.

James Russell and his sons established in the 1860s a firm under that name (James Russell & Sons) and opened branches elsewhere in Sussex, and in the 1880s at several venues in and around London – where he gained commissions form many members of British and European royalty. One of his sons, Thomas (b. 1841) must have found the family firm increasingly claustrophobic (James was father to ten children, six of whom were active in the business), and in the mid-1880s broke away from his siblings, and, living in Cawley Road, set up a rival studio initially in Eastgate, but soon at Southgate also, hence the initial name, Eastgate and Southgate Fine Art Studios, although within a year or so he operated solely from 20 Southgate. There is also a record that the family later operating from 227 Oving Road – which is where one of the present writers lodged when he first came to Chichester!

the family were reluctant, eventually, to maintain the tradition: although Russell's first son, Christopher,[6] continued to run the firm after the death of his father in 1970 for a further 37 years, neither of his children wished to continue – which, in the light of the pressure from national commercial firms and the supermarkets was probably a wise decision. It did, however, close a chapter on Chichester being served by

Fig. 5. Charles Skinner, manager at Purchases during its final decades

a family of shopkeepers who specialized in a trade, who lived within the community they served, and who contributed much to local society.[7]

CODA

Arthur Purchase & Son was not, of course, in the period of its history, the sole vendor of wine in Chichester. Most of the grocers retailed wine also, and a local brewery, actually advertised itself as a 'Wine Merchant'.[8] Further, if one's preference was for beer the opportunities for purchase were immense: in the 1911 Kelly's Directory, there are almost twenty beer retailers listed in Chichester – and that is not counting the numerous public houses.[9]

City records show that wine was being imported through Chichester Harbour as long ago as 1461, for that year Henry VI granted the City a charter to regulate the sale and quality of wine, as well as bread, and beer. Much later it is known that in 1715 there were 50 gallons of Rhenish wine imported to Chichester from Rotterdam, and that about the same time the building we know today as the historic core of Pallant House Gallery was built by Henry Peckham (1683–1764), and that he was commonly known as 'Lisbon' Peckham, owing to his interests in the wine trade.

For sourcing much data given above, we gratefully acknowledge Nancy R. & H. Graham Purchase, Genealogy of the Purchase Family in Britain and Southern Africa (Lulu [www.lulu.com], 2008); and for details of the Russells, www.photohistory-sussex.co.uk/ChichRussellThos.htm - accessed 22.10.2010.

[6] Russell, married at Chichester Cathedral in 1936 by Dean Duncan Jones, had met his future bride, Frances Irene Clarke, at a carol party in Canon Lane on 17 December 1928 – but long engagements were a fashion of the time; Christopher was born 1937, and a second son, Nigel, in 1940.
[7] Russell, for instance, was a City Councillor for many years, and oversaw the celebrations in Chichester associated with the 1951 Festival of Britain; he also prepared a fine account of the loss and recovery of the City's ceremonial plate – see G. A. Russell Purchase, The Story of the Corporation Plate (Chichester 1954).
[8] George Constable, owner of breweries in Arundel and Littlehampton, amalgamated in 1921 with the long-standing Chichester firm of Henty's; the new firm endured until 1954 when Richard Henty, aged only 54, died when cruising on the Queen Mary.
[9] One reason for these numbers relates to the unwholesome water supplies: within Chichester, main sewers were dug barely more than a hundred years ago, in the late 1890s.

6
Personal Attire

Sheila Hale

My Love in her attire does show her wit, it doth so well become her;
For every season she has dressings fit - for winter spring, and summer;
No beauty she doth miss, when all her robes are on;
But beauty's self she is, when all her robes are gone.

(Anon, English Madrigal)

At one time folk would have looked forward to the arrival of the pedlars knocking on the door with trays of pins, threads, a few fabrics and brightly-coloured ribbons with which to repair or freshen last year's hats or dresses. Then there would have been trips to the local towns on market days, dressed in their 'best' clothes – husbands to deliver their animals and enjoy the camaraderie of other farmers, and wives to seek out bargains on clothes for the family and, perhaps, a piece of new fabric to make a dress for herself. Chichester has been well served by drapers, outfitters and clothiers for many a long year. There have been periods of austerity and rationing during the war when it was 'make do and mend', when clothing was patched and repaired, or had pieces 'let in' or 'taken out', or cut down to size for the younger children; when sheets which had gone thin in the centre were turned 'sides to middle' and darned; and pieces of cloth which still had a bit of 'life' in them would be used to make bedcovers in the form of patchwork quilts.

The historic guild of drapers, usually known as the Drapers' Company, has the formal name of The Master and Wardens and Brethren and Sisters of the Guild or Fraternity of the Blessed Mary the Virgin of the Mystery of Drapers of the City of London and received its first Royal Charter in 1364, although an earlier trade association of wool and cloth merchants can be traced back to 1180. Ranking third in the precedence of Livery Companies, the 'Drapers' has provided the City of London with over 100 Mayors.

J. BAKER & CO. LTD, Outfitters, 66 & 66a East Street

These premises were occupied from around 1899 by Fred Longland; also an outfitter, he remained there until 1930. One of his claims to fame was that he was an ardent 'non-drainer' throughout the campaign to install main drainage in East Street. He was vociferous in his opposition and had leaflets printed outlining reasons why 'drainers' would come to regret their decisions![*]

J. Baker & Co. Ltd., took over these premises on the south side of East Street about 1930, almost opposite Bishop's, but they were not to last as long as most of the other traders in this section, closing in the early 1970s. They sold clothing for men and boys. In 1935 the Chichester Players gave a performance in the Assembly Rooms of George Bernard Shaw's *Arms and the Man* and Bakers bought advertising space in the programme, taking advantage of the title of the play thus: "Arms and the Man will receive a PERFECT FIT in LEISURE WEAR at …………"

Morrelli's Café moved into the property in 1973 but currently No 66 is occupied by the Cheltenham & Gloucester Building Society.

BISHOP'S CLOTHING STORES LTD, gents outfitters, 26 East Street

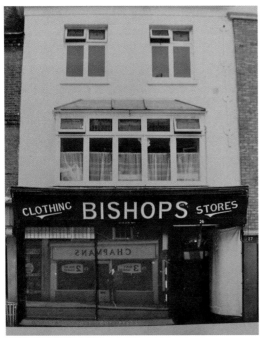

Fig. 1. Bishop's shop front on East Street

Bishop's is another Chichester firm that survived in the same premises for over 100 years! Although there were changes of ownership and in the title of the shop, it retained the founder's name and ethos. In 1887, as a fourteen year old, Harry George Bridger started working in the shop for the Holmes family of tailors and outfitters.

Henry Morley Bishop had been trading as a stationer in Chelsea before opening the above business (which he called H. Bishop) in 1893. Harry G. Bridger acquired the business in 1917 and he remained associated with it until his death in 1951.

Barrington William John Fancy married Harry Bridger's daughter, Ivy, in 1930 and joined the company in 1946, taking over after her father's death. Their son, Keith Fancy, to whom I am indebted for so much information concerning the history of the firm, joined in 1960 and, following the death of his father in 1973, he took over the running of the business.

---

* In fact Chichester was later than many other towns in providing closed drainage and sewage systems, the work not being achieved until the mid-1890s.

Fig. 2. *The advertising light over the entrance*

He described it as a 'middle of the road' gents outfitters. They sold Harris tweed jackets and suits for game-keepers as well as the usual menswear, and had contracts for the supply of uniforms for the Chichester High Schools, for Bishop Luffa, for the Lancastrian and Central schools, and for Phillip Howard School out at Barnham. Mr. Fancy remembers taking stands to gymkhanas and agricultural shows in West Sussex where, as an appointed agent for Harry Hall, the manufacturer of jodhpurs, breeches and other riding equipment, they had the perfect venues for displaying these goods.

Until about the mid-fifties, the firm employed a Company Traveller, Eric Downer. Using a motor-cycle supplied by the company, he would travel around local villages – Selsey, Compton, Singleton and the like – on regular days of the week, taking orders one week and delivering the goods the following. Some orders, if the goods were urgently required, were parcelled up and put onto the local bus for delivery.

They were long days in the shop, particularly so when it was time to change the window display. On the other side of the road at Nos. 66 & 66a were their competitors, J. Baker & Co. Ltd., and Bishop's would wait for Bakers window to be dressed before completing their own so that they might be able to display better bargains.

With the advent of the 'multiples', and rising rates, it became more difficult for the business to survive and impossible to keep prices competitive. Therefore the business closed in 1994 and the property was sold.

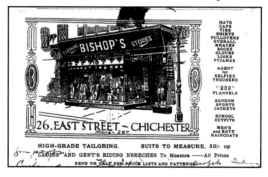

Fig. 3. *Letterhead (detail c. 1893)*

CHARGE & CO., linen draper, silk mercer and clothier, 74 & 75 South Street; baby linen, 14 South Street

In January 1775 the marriage of Benjamin Charge and Olive Goodyer was solemnized at St. Andrew's Church (Oxmarket). They were destined to become the founders of the well-known and highly respected family of high class drapers in Chichester through to the 20th century. Benjamin Charge, a saddler, and his wife, set-up home in Little London where they had five sons and four daughters all of whom were baptized at St. Andrew's.

Fig. 4. Charge at No. 1 South Street (renumbered as 74/75)

Over a century ago, in a Post Office Directory, the firm is described as linen drapers, silk mercers and clothiers. The store has always been family run with the assistance of an extensive staff. The ground floor accommodated general and furnishing drapery, linen, silks and haberdashery. The first floor housed the showrooms for coats and dresses, with millinery; a department catering for weddings; plus a department for family mourning clothes and accessories with the pledge to 'execute orders promptly'. At no. 14 South Street, (on the west side of the street) the premises leased from the Dean & Chapter were used for baby linens until this shop closed in 1964, and the lease was taken on by Maurice Evans and Jean Siviter for their floristry business – Hoopers of Chichester. Over the years various members of the Charge family have been listed as trading at other addresses for instance at 26 East Street (later Bishop's Clothing Stores Ltd.) and at 63 South Street (later, G. M. Turnbull).

Charges were ahead of their times for they were one of the first Chichester businesses to take advantage of a filmed advertisement which was played between feature films in the local cinemas during the 1950s. When the commentator reached the words 'Charges of Chichester close by the Cross' there would always be hoots and laughter from the audience.

When Ernest Edward Charge married Ellen Burgess, one of his shop assistants, in 1912, one of the sons from their marriage was Ernest A. P. Charge, born in 1913, who was to become the final Director. He succeeded his widowed mother and aunt and continued to run the business until his retirement in 1968 – the end of an era, at which time he sold the premises to the Midland Bank. After the death of his first wife he remarried. Peter Charge, as he was always known, died in 1996 at the age of 83 years.

HENRY DENYER, draper, 84 North Street

Henry Denyer was born in Chichester in 1856 and was in business as a draper from the late 1880s. He and his wife Anne, had several children. One son, Charles Leonard Denyer, chose to become a school teacher and went to work in Colchester; Evelyn Annie Denyer, aged 25, and her 12 year old brother, were living with their widowed mother in 5 Guildhall Street in 1911; whilst the third son, Henry John Ryan Denyer and his wife had taken over the drapery business and were living on the premises.

Fig. 5. Denyer's premises

Ten years earlier Henry J. R. had been working in a large drapery firm at 78-83 North Street, Brighton, where he was just one of sixteen drapers' assistants living-in. This experience must have proved invaluable when his father died and he had to take over the business in Chichester. Mr. Denyer often caused embarrassment to his customers, especially young girls accompanying their older relatives, for he had the habit of bounding forward as the door opened and enquiring what 'Madam' was looking for, then, no matter how intimate the item of clothing required, he would call an assistant and loudly announce 'Madam's' request to the 'world', or at least to everyone in the shop!

During the Second World War he was a member of the Civil Defence (Post West 5 at Parklands) and is shown in a photograph in Bernard Price's *Chichester: The Valiant Years* (1978). Mr. Denyer is at one end of the back row and Mr. Penney, another draper from North Street, at the other.

The business is still listed at this address in 1954 but does not appear in the 1964 Directory. In 2011 the premises are occupied by a 'fashion draper', Accessorize.

DOMANS FASHIONS LTD, ladies outfitters and costumiers, 24 North Street

William Doman, the founder of the well-known drapery firm, opened his first business in East Street in 1868 (see page 112) and is shown to have a second shop in North Street by 1874. William Heath Doman, his son, followed him into the businesses which then traded as Doman & Son.

William Heath Doman married Maud Alice Vick (daughter of a local builder from Tower Street) in 1899. When William died in 1948, their two sons took over and decided to split the business into two separate enterprises according to their individual expertise. Denzil Robert Doman (known as Dick or Dicky) took the East Street premises and further

Fig. 6. Doman's store in North Street sporting SALE notices!

developed the soft furnishings, whilst Arthur Cedric Doman took 24 North Street which was selling lingerie at that time and developed it into a ladies outfitters and costumiers.

In the fifties, when the fashion was for sheepskin coats, Arthur Cedric made it his business to become a specialist in that field, word spread, and customers came from near and far to purchase these garments. As the fashions changed so, of course, did the stock of dresses, skirts, suits and coats which were always of good quality, and sold by a pleasant staff.

Denzil Robert Doman, his wife (née Bastow), and family lived on the first and second floors of his brother's North Street shop and at least one of their sons was born there. During the Second World War when the siren sounded, the family would dash down to the shop where there was an Anderson shelter which they shared with the staff and, presumably, any customers who might have been in the shop at the time of the air raid.

Towards the end of the 1960s, Arthur Cedric Doman, whose home was in Midhurst, decided to retire and sell the business at no. 24. However, it was not long before he realised that he had retired too soon and bought a general store in Fernhurst (nothing at all to do with fashion or furnishing). He kept that store for a further few years before retiring for a second time.

Fig. 7. Dunn's expansive premises in South Street with staff

DUNN & SON (Dunn's Cheap Drapery Bazaar), 72 & 73 South Street

Alfred Dunn founded this store around 1862. He and his wife, Caroline, had seven children, some of whom worked in the business, along with four drapers' assistants and two apprentices, plus a housekeeper and a domestic servant (1881). The business continued as Dunn & Son (Drapers, Chichester) Ltd., until the late 1950s or early 1960s and one wonders how so many similar large drapery businesses survived in a relatively small city. Stead & Simpson Ltd., the shoe retailers, have occupied the same premises up to the present time.

G. A. GEERING, draper, haberdasher and milliner, 78/79/80 North Street

Whenever the name of this store is mentioned the first memory people express is that of the overhead wire railway for transferring cash. Customers purchases having been completed, the shop assistant put the bill and money into a cup, screwed it into the top half which was attached to the rail, pulled a lever or cord and the whole thing began its journey up and across the ceiling to the cashier who sat in an elevated cubicle. Having retrieved the bill and cash, the receipt and any change were replaced in the cup, screwed up, and then began its return journey across the store and back to the counter arriving with a satisfactory 'ping'! Numerous systems were developed and patented in America in the 1880s as a

Fig. 8. Geering's decorated for Christmas

more secure method of handling cash than the use of cash registers around the store. It was not long before their use spread to the United Kingdom, and they were particularly favoured by drapery and grocery businesses and department stores, though it is thought that Geerings was the only store to deploy such a system in Chichester.

In some modern supermarkets an updated system of pneumatic tubes are used today as a safe way of transporting rolls of notes and loose change to and from the tills, and larger ones are used in some hospitals for the transportation of medical records around the wards, and for taking various samples directly from the Operating Theatres to the Pathology Laboratory but they don't have the romance of the overhead cash 'railways' of Geerings!!

George Albert Geering, and his wife Kate, started his business at 78 North Street in the early 1900s, taking over the drapery business of Charles Rees. The firm gradually expanded into the neighbouring properties no. 79 (a confectioner) and no. 80 (formerly the Wheatsheaf Inn). With its prominent position either side of the Crooked 'S' (Shambles Alley) leading to St. Martin's Street, it was a popular store and one which gave good value for money.

Fig. 9. Interior of Geering's

There was a change of ownership in c.1950/1951, when Mr. Desmond Cockayne took over. In 1953 no. 78 was occupied by William Clark & Sons, decorators merchants. The remainder of the store continued to trade under the familiar name, and in 1973 it was listed as Geerings (Chichester) Ltd., departmental store.

In 2011 no. 78 houses Macari's coffee shop; no.79 Between the Lines, gifts and cards; and no. 80, Robert Dyas, electrical and household goods.

PARVINS, ladies' fashions, 56 East Street

In 1913 these premises were occupied by Mr. C. Hoare, a baker, but in 1920 we find Parvins, Costumiers (next door to Mr. T. Humphrey, tobacconist, on the corner of St. John's Street).

Mrs. Emily J. Parvin was a dressmaker, and the founder of the business which sold rather smart coats and suits. It is a name that older Cicestrian's remember, as well as the position of the shop, but that is the extent of their knowledge and it seems impossible to find documentary evidence other than in the Directories where the business is still listed in 1971. The site is now occupied by Harrington Leather and Travel Goods.

Fig. 10. Mrs Parvin's shop, nestling between the tobacconist and Adcock's garage

H. PENNEY & CO. LTD, drapers, 73 North Street

The Penney family were well-established drapers in Portsea, Portsmouth, when one of their sons, Harry, came to Chichester and set-up a drapery business at the above address c. 1878. In 1881 at the age of 26, he is shown as a draper employing 15 persons, three of whom were living on the premises, a milliner, a draper's salesman and a draper's apprentice.

The property, tucked in beside the Council Chamber on the east side of North Street, was an attractive building which was occupied by various generations of the same family for over seventy years until the business moved to smaller premises at 60 East Street where they survived until after 1973. As well as being drapers, they were ladies outfitters, milliners, and sold household linens and soft furnishings. The North Street site is now occupied by Dorothy Perkins.

Fig. 11. Penney & Co., adjacent to the Council House in North Street

GUY REYNOLDS, gentlemen's outfitters, 77 North Street

Alfred Reynolds had started his Chichester business as a hatter and hosier at 84 East Street by 1899 although he may have been there before this date. He owned a second shop in the Arcade at Bognor Regis, a corner site onto the High Street. After the death of his first wife, Alfred re-married and they had a son, Dennis, a half-brother to Guy. Dennis took no part in the business.

Guy Reynolds had taken over the firm by 1927, and a bill head for 1st June, 1934 reads: 'Guy Reynolds. Hatter; Tailor; Hosier; Glover; Evening dress wear; Sports wear; Showroom first floor; Lincoln Bennett & Co's Celebrated Hats and Caps; Sole Agent for Burberry, Bowfield and Zambrom Coats and Jaeger Co. Ltd., Celebrated Men's Wear Productions.'

During the early 1930s, Guy Reynolds moved the business to leasehold property at 77 North Street where it remained until the

Fig. 12. Alfred Reynolds' window (detail) – at 84 East Street

owner sold the premises to a Kidderminster Property Company in 1987, who bought the firm out.

The building was actually divided into two parts, two-thirds occupied by Guy Reynolds, and one-third by Whitehead & Sons, watchmakers. Peter Burnand, to whom I am indebted for giving me so much of this information, first worked for Guy Reynolds as a shop boy, running errands etc. on his bicycle, long before the streets were pedestrianized, so traffic still went through the city. Everybody stood their bicycles against the pavement kerbs, but he had to be careful not to leave his outside Mr Whitehead's third of the building or risk being told off!

In 1957 Peter was employed as a full-time assistant who obviously proved a great asset because in 1965 he was made a Director. In 1968 after the death of Guy Reynolds, his son, Arthur, continued to run the business until his retirement in 1985 at which time, he asked Peter Burnand to buy him out. Sadly, Peter and his wife, Margaret, were only to be Managing Directors until October 1987 when the Property Company bought them out.

At some time during the late 1950s and early 1960s, D. Combes (Garden and Pet Supplies) Ltd., moved into 76 North Street (formerly occupied by Whitehead & Son) and decided to do some alterations. Their builder hadn't realised that part of the floor of 76 was immediately over one of the showrooms of 77, not, that is, until his pick-axe broke through the ceiling of the room below and he found himself looking into a completely different shop!

So many of the local businessmen and women joined in the social life of the city and Guy Reynolds was no exception. The Chichester Players was founded in 1933 following a Public Meeting, and a programme for their performance of George Bernard Shaw's *Arms and the Man* given at the Assembly Room in May 1935, lists Guy Reynolds as Wardrobe Master, as does the one for the October performance of *The Rose without a Thorn* in the same year. The programmes make interesting reading and show the support given by the business community, whether as performers (actors, musicians, producers, directors and conductors), behind the scenes, or by buying advertising space in the programme, or loaning furniture and other stage props.

ALFRED SYKES & SON LTD, drapers, 9 & 10 South Street

Henry Gadd (brother of Thomas Gadd, master grocer in Northgate) leased the premises from the Trustees of St. Mary's Hospital and set up a wholesale and retail drapers shop on the site in 1845.

Michael Turnbull came to Chichester in 1862, taking over the above business and later establishing an outfitters shop at 62 & 63 South Street. When his son, George M. Turnbull, succeeded his father, he took Alfred Sykes, who had already been associated with the drapery side of the business, into partnership and it became Turnbull & Sykes. G. M. Turnbull, outfitters, and Turnbull & Sykes, drapers, were two separate businesses but both occupied imposing premises almost opposite each other in South Street.

This partnership was dissolved during World War 1 and Alfred's son, Leonard Sykes, joined the business. In 1915 Leonard married Constance Kimbell, sister of William Kimbell, baker,

Fig. 13. Alfred Sykes at South Street

87

confectioner and caterer (see 'Bread and Confectionery). Between the wars a dressmaker and six seamstresses were employed to make up coats and dresses from fabrics chosen by the customers from stock. Eight members of staff lived over the shop and a cook/housekeeper and domestic servant were employed to cater for them.

When Leonard Sykes son, Peter, came out of Naval Service in 1946, he joined the business, taking over in 1967. In an interview with Edward Brown for the *Chichester Observer* some years later, he recalls that 'Chichester was a happy place to do business. Though there were half-a-dozen similar shops within a short distance, there was no animosity. Rivalry was friendly'. When, in 1959, they decided to concentrate on dressmaking materials and millinery, the shop was divided, the south side being taken by Peter Lord shoes (now Rohde Shoes).

During the 1950s and 1960s it was a very popular pastime among young girls to spend Saturday afternoons poring over the Butterick, Style, and Vogue catalogues in the shop searching for dressmaking patterns to suit one's shape and then choosing the appropriate fabrics. Having also purchased matching threads, bias bindings, buttons and zips, we scurried home to pin the pattern onto the fabric. In no time it was cut out, pinned, basted, adjusted to fit and then sewn together over the weekend. What fun we had, even if our garments didn't always look exactly as shown on the model on the front of the pattern! As the price of fabrics and patterns increased and cheaper imports of ready made clothing became available, it was no longer economical to make one's own clothes.

When Peter Sykes retired in 1982, Alan Austin, who had had his own fabric businesses in Godalming and Farnham, took over and the name became Austin-Sykes. It remained in these premises until the lease was due for renewal in 1989 when it moved to temporary accommodation in the Old Theatre along the road, whilst waiting for work on the shop they had acquired in St. Pancras to be completed. The St. Pancras business closed in 2004 and is now occupied by an undertaker.

G. M. TURNBULL, outfitters, 62 & 63 South Street

Mr. Michael Turnbull came to Chichester in 1862 taking over the business of Henry Gadd, draper at 9 & 10 South Street and later also established this other business as a hosier and outfitter on the opposite side of the road. (The early history is already rehearsed at the start of the preceding entry). Although Mr. Turnbull had started his business of hosier and gentlemen's outfitter at 62 South Street (currently Bon Marché), in 1892 he describes himself as a tailor and hatter, and is selling shirts, ties, boots and

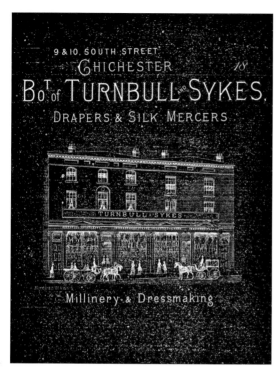

Fig. 14. Promotion literature for Turnbull and Sykes

shoes. His trade quickly expanded into the adjoining premises. As well as being known for his high class woollens, he specialised in rugged looking 'Bulldog' shirts favoured by workmen and the appealing wooden bulldog model in the shop proved an interesting talking point among his customers.

George M. Turnbull was elected Mayor of Chichester in 1909 and in his acceptance speech he asked what qualifications are needed to do the job well: '… does he need [he asked] to be a good footballer, a good photographer, or should he be fond of bowls?'! He must have found the correct answer because he was re-elected in 1910 and 1911, and, again in 1919. In a newspaper cutting from his scrapbook, he is described as having been a useful citizen, with his connection with the Finance and Education Committees of the Corporation having been particularly valuable. It was also reported that for 12 years he sat continuously on the Council and that since Councillor Turnbull was appointed a Commissioner of the Peace, he has been a regular attendant at Petty Sessions. In 1923 he was elected Mayor of the St. Pancras Corporation.

After serving in India during the war, Leslie Turnbull returned to Chichester and joined his father in the business in c.1920. Turnbull's continued on this site until being sold c.1964. In 2011 it is occupied by Bon Marché, ladies clothing.

7

FORK'ANDLES – CHICHESTER'S LOST IRONMONGERS & DECORATORS' MERCHANTS

ALAN H. J. GREEN

The traditional British ironmonger's shop was immortalized in the famous Two Ronnies sketch in which Ronnie Barker plays a customer in Ronnie Corbett's shop. The sketch revolves around a series of misunderstandings; the customer's request for 'fork 'andles' being misunderstood as 'four candles' - and so on in similar vein. Ronnie Corbett is dressed in a long brown work coat and produces the requested goods with amazing celerity from behind the counter, in both of which he typifies the ironmonger's shops that were once to be found in Chichester. These shops supplied the building trade and individual customers with equal efficiency and their brown-coated assistants had an encyclopaedic knowledge of everything they stocked - and what it was for.

Overlapping ironmongers in trade to a certain extent, and very similar in ethos, were the decorators' merchants who stocked paints, wallpapers, putty, glass and all the tools of the decorator's craft.

As well as being proverbial Aladdin's caves for the cognoscenti, all these shops had a most distinctive smell, of creosote mingling with coconut matting, of linseed oil blending with dustbin powder. With everything in today's equivalent shops being pre-packaged, these heady aromas have disappeared.

All the ironmongers in the district were members of the Ironmongers' Association which used to organize meetings at the Dolphin & Anchor Hotel in Chichester. At these meetings suppliers would announce their latest products to the trade and dispense generous hospitality as well. The meetings provided a forum for rival firms to meet socially and indulge in what is now known as 'networking' within what was a fairly close-knit area of the retail trade.[1]

Although all the firms were rivals, there was much cooperation between them and it was standard practice to help each other out. If, in fulfilling customer orders, a particular item was out of stock, one of the shop boys would be sent running to another establishment to collect the missing item, generally whilst the customer waited. [2]

During the 1950s and 60s my father, Wilfred Green, traded as a carpenter and decorator from our house in Orchard Street, and had accounts at most of these businesses. As a boy I was a frequent visitor to them when running errands, feeling very important when I charged things to his account.

---

1 Told to the author by Brain Clear who attended these functions when working for Jay's and Ray's.
2 Told to the author by several of the former employees he interviewed.

HALSTED & SONS, 81/82 East Street

Although *Baker's Dozen* is focused on businesses that have closed since 1950, mention must be made at the outset of the earliest of Chichester ironmongers, Halsted & Sons, who closed in 1936. The business was started in the 1820s in East Street by Charles Halsted, a plumber and decorator, whose three sons took it on to new heights through the 1840s by developing an extensive iron and brass foundry, together with a sheet metal works, between North and East Pallants – the site now occupied by the Baffin's Lane car park. Here they made kitchen ranges, pumps, domestic ironwork, farm implements, street furniture and even steam engines. The East Street shop was rebuilt in 1905 / 06 (currently occupied by Pia and CC) and had a two-level showroom in which much of the stock had been made around the corner in the foundry. Halsted's foundry closed in 1932 and the shop four years later. The foundry buildings lingered on in other uses until 1960 when they were flattened by the City Council to form the present car park.[3] Fortunately the shop building survives and in the keystone over its central window the Halsted logo - a key - can still be seen. Halsted's shop has all but passed out of living memory but here and there around the city can still be found gulley gratings, fence posts and stopcock covers bearing the legend 'Halsted & Sons, Chichester'.[4]

Pau Foster

T. E. JAY, 7 & 8 East Street

Facing Halsted's across East Street was their fiercest rival, T. E. Jay, whose extensive shop was on the site now occupied by HMV. This business also went back to the 19th

Fig. 1. A view of the frontage of T. E. Jay's shop taken in 1958. Above the unifying fascia it can be seen that the shop comprised two very different Georgian houses. In the left hand shop window is an array of spades, shovels and forks - with their requiste 'andles(!) - and in the right hand first floor window there appears to be a lifebelt, typifying the wide range of goods on offer

---

[3] Green, Alan H. J. *Halsted & Sons of Chichester. Sussex Industrial History,* Issue 35, pp 2-13. Sussex Industrial Archaeology Society, 2005.

[4] The author had a few retired Halsted products in his garden.

Fig. 2. T. E. Jay's shop pictured in the 1950s.
Standing in front are, left to right, Harold Linkhorn,
Ken Clark, Herbert Webberly (Clerk) and Jim
Turner. Note that, apart from the clerk who wears
a suit, they are all sporting the obligatory brown
work-coat.

century, having been founded by Frederick Adames who was trading as an ironmonger as early as 1869.[5] In 1871 he was trading in partnership with Thomas Grant as *Adames & Grant* and when their premises were valued in 1875 the workshops contained three forges and an iron store which suggests that, although not founders, they made or repaired wrought iron work.[6] Directories show that by 1880 Adames was trading alone as 'Frederick Adames – late Adames and Grant' advertising himself as 'ironmonger, iron, oil and colour merchant' and listing lawn mowers, heating apparatus, agricultural implements and pumps amongst his stock in trade. When Adames died in 1885 his business was taken over by the splendidly named Adolphus Ballard.[7] Ballard served as mayor of Chichester in 1896/7 and was also the author of a famous history of Chichester that was first published in 1896.

In 1905 the business was sold to T. E. Jay in whose family name it was to last for 54 years; the largest ironmongers between Portsmouth and Brighton and one of Chichester's greatest institutions. The premises were large, extending back as far as the Market House to the north and round the back of neighbouring shops into St Martin's Street to the east. The courtyard at the rear of the shop, where the workshops were situated, was accessible from North Street via the now-lost Swan Lane which ran alongside the Market House. Below the shop were extensive cellars whither, when the shop was busy, trade customers were directed to seek out what they wanted, but were frequently unable to find their way out again as the staircase was hidden in an alcove. Search parties had to be sent to rescue them.[8]

Jay's stocked everything one could wish for and also provided the services of locksmith, tinsmith, agricultural machinery and lawnmower repair and marine engineering. This was all supported by a clerical section run by Herbert Webberly with Mr Low as accountant. From 1954 the yacht chandlery department was listed in directories as *Jay's Marine (T. E. Jay)* with a separate address in St Martin's Street, next door to the *Hole in the Wall* public house.

The concept of self-service was unheard of in those days; instead customers queued at a long counter to be served by one of the six assistants who would disappear to seek

[5] WSRO AddMS 32886 lease of 8 Little London to Frederick Adames 29 September 1869 in which he is described as *ironmonger.*
[6] WSRO AddMS 25092 Valuer's notebook (Wyatt & Co) dated 4 May 1875
[7] WSRO AddMS 41259 A collection of election material containing a printed notice for a vacancy on Chichester City Council 'in consequence of the death of the lamented Mr Frederick Adames'
[8] Told to the author by Brian Clear, a former Jay's employee

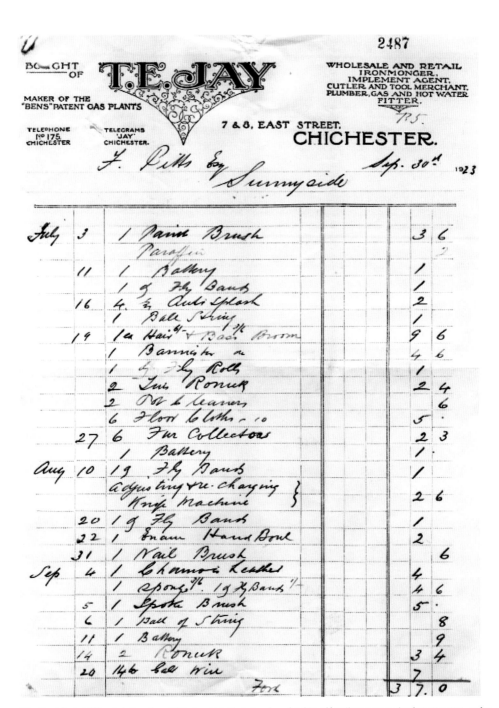

Fig. 3. *A Jay's bill head, dating from 1923, in which T. E. Jay describes himself as 'ironmonger, implement agent, cutler and tool merchant, plumber and gas and hot water fitter. Mr F. Pitt's purchases, which went on to a second page, included brushes, paraffin, furniture polish, batteries and string, and he had also had his knife-polishing machine adjusted. Over the three months his bill amounted to £3 8s 10d.*

out all their requirements from the stores. Completing a large order could take up to half an hour.

Jay's was a family business, one of many in Chichester, and the last owner, Thomas Jay, served his city as a magistrate and was heavily involved with the Rotary Club. Mr Jay is remembered as being a kind and generous man who looked after his staff and provided free 'works outings' to London or Brighton to see a show and enjoy a meal.[9] In March 1959 Thomas Jay announced his intention to retire, close the business and leave Chichester.[10] He had wanted to convert the premises into a shopping mall but, since the City Council refused planning permission for this venture, and knowing that the council did not approve of the new-fangled supermarkets, he sold the premises instead to Tesco for £46,000. A huge closing-down sale, lasting several months, was held which on its first day alone raised £500.[11] The staff dispersed to other similar businesses in the area but two left to set up their own ironmongery businesses with generous assistance from Mr Jay.

The empty shop was used temporarily by Lennard's shoe shop whilst their premises on the corner of North and East Streets were being rebuilt, but was then demolished and a new Tesco supermarket was built on the site.[12]

On its closure in 1959 this legendary East Street ironmongers business, which had been trading for some 90 years, had seen off its rival Halsted's by 23 years and no doubt benefited from inheriting their former farming customers. The yacht chandlery section in St Martin's Street continued as a separate business, run by Mr Ken Clark as *Jay's Marine* and managed to survive even after a disastrous fire gutted the premises in 1964.

David Messam joined Jay's from school, rising to become the specialist buyer of tools, and after the closure he used his expertise to set up his own tool shop. This opened in 1959 at 28 East Street, a small shop owned by his wife's family who had been trading there as the drapers G. E. Lever. Mr Jay, with typical generosity, provided much of the starting stock.[13] Happily this well-stocked tool and ironmongery shop is still run by the Messam family; it is one of the few independent businesses left in Chichester and provides a positive link with Jay's.

G. PINE, Eastgate Square

There must have been something about East Street that attracted ironmongers for in Eastgate Square was another much-missed firm, that of G. Pine. This business too goes back a long way having been established in 1843 by Mr H Light on the east side of the

[9]   Ibid.
[10] *Chichester Observer 22 March 1959.*
[11] Brown, Edward, *Chichester in the 1950s* E B Publications, Chichester 1996. Page 14 contains a short article about the demise of Jay's arising from an interview with the son of the last owner.
[12] *Chichester Observer* 19 September 1959, a report about the sale to Tesco.
[13] Told to the author by Mrs Margaret Messam, wife of the late David Messam.

square at No. 9, next to the *Unicorn* public house. Light also had a store on the south side of the square, next to the *Cattle Market Inn*. Gilbert Pine bought Light's business in 1913 and in 1928 transferred the shop to the stores premises across the square[14]. Strangely, once there, Pine's shop never acquired a street number, directories simply listing it as being between The *Cattle Market Inn* (No 13) and a gentleman's outfitter's shop at No. 14.

Gilbert Pine died in 1941 and the business was taken over by his son Bob.[15] From the early 1950s Bob Pine progressively extended the premises round behind the Cattle Market Inn into Market Road, where he had bought a row of four cottages. Two of the cottages were converted to shops but later demolished to make way for the two-storey building now occupied by *Blockbuster Video*, however the other two had to be spared as the tenants refused to move out.[16] The last piece of extension was over a yard next to The Bull Inn, which housed the garden machinery department.

Fig. 4. *Pine's shop in 1965, shewing the main entrance in Eastgate Square. The window is crammed full but could only give prospective customers a hint of what might be found inside. The Cattle Market Inn to the left is a pub no more.*

As well as the usual ironmongery, Pine's stocked a wide range of general household goods such as crockery and also branched out into those fitted kitchens that had become *de rigueur* in the 1970s. These were sold in an upstairs showroom, the favoured make being *Gold Pine*. Pine's shop contained the busy Eastgate Post Office which was one

[14] CDM. A 'timeline' produced for an exhibition about Pine's in 1990 using information supplied by Bob Pine, the then owner.
[15] WSRO MP1966 The manuscript of an adult education project into Chichester businesses (n/d but *c.*1979) by Mr B Winch. Pine's was then still in business and he interviewed members of the Pine family who supplied much of the information.
[16] Told to the author by Vince Foote, a former employee of Pine's.

of several sub-post offices to be found in the city at the time. The shop also stocked specialist tools and regularly advertised this fact in *The Martlet*, the magazine of Chichester High School for Boys where, between 1955 and 1969, they were offering a Myford ML7 lathe for 'under £45'. The price never increased so they either found a magical way of containing inflation or simply did not bother to update the advert!

The extended shop was somewhat rambling and had a basement as well as the upstairs showroom, but the 20-plus staff were always very helpful and knew precisely where everything was. In Pine's, if you only wanted one six inch nail you could buy just one six inch nail. In the 1970s Bob Pine, following the national trend, introduced an element of self-service in the shop but regretted it on account of the amount of stock that was lifted by some light-fingered 'customers'.

MYFORD LATHES
a first in everything

This precision lathe is ahead of all others. No other lathe offers you so much. Thousands of satisfied users will tell you of its many advantages.

● Over sixty accessories available—just when you want them. You buy only what you want. You buy no accessories that you have no use for.

You can buy a MYFORD ML7 for less than **£45**

EASTGATE SQUARE, CHICHESTER Phone 2232

Remember **PINES** *for MYFORDS*

Fig. 5. Pines regularly advertised in The Martlet, *the magazine of Chichester High School for Boys. Here, in 1962, they offer a Myford ML7 lathe for less than £45. Notice how the address contains no shop number – they never had one!*

Bob Pine was renowned for being somewhat irascible to staff and customers alike who displeased him, and it was noticeable that when Jay's closed none of the staff wished to take up his job offers! On the other hand though, he was generally fair and could be very kind to staff who served him well.[17] In addition to his business acumen Bob Pine was a very skilled artist and every year he produced a calendar for his account customers which carried an exquisite drawing of a Chichester scene. My father always had a Pine calendar hanging over his desk, but regrettably neither he nor I thought to keep one. When Bob Pine bought a new delivery van one member of staff, Vince Foote, suggested that, instead of traditional lettering it be adorned with a large version of a Pine's calendar – and this was done, surely creating the most distinctive delivery van in Chichester.

Pines closed in 1990, having gone into liquidation in April of that year.[18] Their demise caused great sorrow amongst Cicestrians, and the sale of their stock was long and drawn out owing to the vast quantity of goods that had to be cleared. The buildings still stand, but have been much divided up, the main shop in Eastgate Square is now *Fired Earth* whilst the rearmost portion on Market Road is a Chinese restaurant.

---

[17] Told to the author by Michael Timlick and Geoff Kent, former employees of Pine's.
[18] *The London Gazette* of 10 April 1990 carried the public notice of the liquidation.

JUPP & LAKER, 45 North Street

One would have thought that with two large ironmongers – Jay's and Pine's – there would not have been room for another, but at 45 North Street Messrs Jupp and Laker opened one such in 1949. Harold Laker had joined Pine's on discharge form the army but left to set out in business with Mr Jupp who had previously worked for Stride's, the auctioneers. Unfortunately, having failed to capture a large enough slice of the market, Jupp & Laker only lasted until 1958 when it closed down. The premises then became a florist's shop which also housed the Northgate post office.[19]

Fig. 6. *Jupp & Laker, North Street*

RAY'S HARDWARE, 68 North Street

Fig. 7. *Ray's Hardware shop at 68 North Street, pictured in 1965. The 'No Waiting' sign does not enhance the view, but the fine Georgian door-case will be noted*

Another refugee from the closure of Jay's in 1959 was Ray Chatfield, who was the senior buyer.[20] In March of that year he applied to the Trustees of St John's Chapel to take on the lease of 68 North Street, formerly the dental surgery of Mr Alex Roberts, and submitted a planning application to the City Council to turn it into a shop. In June 1959 the lease was sealed and, having obtained planning permission, Mr Chatfield opened *Ray's Hardware*. As with David Messam, Ray Chatfield received generous support from Thomas Jay in provision of his starting stock and Thomas Jay even acted as witness to the lease of 68 North Street.[21] The business is described in the directories as 'hardware merchants and ironmongers' in which areas he focused, leaving specialist tool sales to his erstwhile Jay's colleague David Messam. With his experience as a buyer, Ray Chatfield knew where to procure the more obscure items requested by his customers and would generally have them available next day.[22] In 1962 he extended the shop back by annexing some outbuildings and linking them to the main shop.

---

[19] Jupp & Laker first appear in an advertisement in the City Guide of 1949. They also advertised in *The Martlet up to 1958*.
[20] Told to the author by Mrs Margaret Messam.
[21] WSRO Par 39/102 St John's Trustee's Minute Book 1903-1985.
[22] Told to the author by Brain Clear who worked at Ray's Hardware following the closure of Jay's.

Unfortunately, owing to serious illness, Ray Chatfield had to give up the business in 1969 and transferred it to Mr D G Jeffery who had been trading as a builder.[23] After this time the shop gave the impression of not being particularly well-stocked, especially on the ironmongery side. However Mr Jeffrey frequently undercut Woolworths on household goods and I remember in the 1970s being directed by a Woolworth's employee to Ray's to buy a dustbin, as they were cheaper!

Ray's Hardware closed down in 1988 and the ground floor of 68 North Street is currently occupied by *Coral the Bookmaker*.

J H SMURTHWAITE, 39 North Street

All ironmongers' shops carried stocks of paints, brushes and sandpaper (as we have seen the mighty Halsted empire started with decorating) but their ranges were too limited for professional decorators whose needs were met by specialist decorator's merchants. The oldest established - and longest lived - of these was J H Smurthwaite. The business was founded by Israel Smurthwaite, who came to Chichester from Yorkshire in the 1850s. He set up his business at 39 North Street in 1857 as an oil and colour merchant: in those days decorators would mix their own paint from oil and ground pigments. In 1912 Israel died and left the business to his son Benjamin who died in 1928 passing it on in turn to his son Herbert, and eventually to Herbert's widow Hilda.[24] Although by this time Smurthwaite's were stocking the full range of decorating materials and tools, including wallpaper, as late as the 1933 they were still (misleadingly) listed in the Chichester Directories as simply 'oil and colour merchants'.

Fig. 8. *The frontage of Smurthwaite's shop at 39 North Street in 1980. In those days shops prominently displayed the street number, something that rarely happens today. The glass department was in a courtyard at the rear of the premises.*

Where Smurthwaite's scored over their rivals was in the supply of glass and they had a separate building to the rear where all grades and sizes of window glass would be cut to order. They also supplied paraffin which was dispensed from a pump in the middle

23 WSRO Par39/106 Legal documents relating to the lease of 68 North Street by the St John's Trustees.
24 WSRO MP1966 op. cit.

Fig. 9. *The interior of Smurthwaite's shop following the takeover by Brewer & Sons. The paraffin pump is still in situ but by now it had been isolated, doubtless having come to the attention of the fire officer. Beyond the shelves of paint could be found the wallpaper displays and, right at the back, the door leading out to the glass department.*

Fig. 10. *Smurthwaite's c. 1984. From left to right, Bob Ewins, Ted Lee, Les Wood, manager (formerly glass-cutter). Although the Brewers' logo is on the wall the shop was still trading as Smurthwaite at this time.*

of the shop into customers' own cans, something that would horrify today's fire officers. In the days before central heating became widespread, many houses were heated by oil stoves and there were two main brands of paraffin on offer, *Esso Blue* and *Aladdin Pink* – Smurthwaite's stocked the latter. Well into the 1970s, when such practices were decidedly old-fashioned, Smurthwaite's were still selling white lead and decorator's pigments (colours), trimming wallpapers and dispensing loose linseed oil from a tank in their basement. Another old-fashioned effect still noticeable at this time was the drop off in trade during Goodwood Week when many building firms closed down for the duration![25]

Mrs Smurthwaite, who was much revered, left the running of the business to Leslie Edbury and Fred Smith both of whom were long-term employees, the former having joined in 1930. Leslie Edbury had been a trustee of St John's Chapel, with which his family had had a long association, until it closed in 1973.[26] When Mrs Smurthwaite died in 1974 she left the business to Messrs Edbury and Smith who continued to run it for a further six years as J. H. Smurthwaite.[27]

In 1980 Leslie Ebury and Fred Smith sold the business to the Eastbourne-based chain of decorators' merchants, C. Brewer & Sons, who not only retained the Smurthwaite name, but also restored the fascia to Israel Smurthwaite's[28] ornate Victorian design, for which they received a heritage award. When the lease on 39 North Street expired, Brewers moved to new and much larger premises next to the bypass in Oving, which opened in 1987. On the move the Smurthwaite name was dropped, and 39 North Street became a ladies' outfitters.

WILLIAM CLARK & SONS / R. R. PERRY & SONs, 78 North Street

Although my father bought his glass and paraffin from Smurthwaite's, he chose to buy the rest of his decorating supplies from William Clark and Sons, whose North Street premises were on the north side of Shambles Alley (the Crooked S). Clarks were agents for all the principal brands of paint, including the now-vanished names *Duradio*, *Brolac*, and *Walpamur*, and stocked a wide range of wallpapers. They had hefty wallpaper sample books that customers could borrow to take home in order to see the papers in their rooms before choosing. William Clark took over his father's painting and decorating business at 41 South Street in 1920 but from 1929 he is listed in the directories as being a paint merchant, obviously having undergone a career change.[29] William Clark moved the business to 78 North Street in 1953 having taken over premises that

[25] Told to the author by Les Woods who joined Smurthwaite's from school in 1973 aged 15. He is now manager of Brewer's Portsmouth Branch.
[26] WSRO Par 39/102 op. cit.
[27] Welsh, Paddy *Fifty Years at Smurthwaite's an interview with Leslie William Edbury, aged 85.* Article in *Chichester History No 16*, Chichester Local History Society 1999.
[28] By the 1933 directory the name had changed from I. Smurthwaite to J. H. Smurthwaite.
[29] Chichester directories from the early 20th century chart the change from H. Clark & Son to W. Clark.

Fig. 11. *William Clark and Sons, decorators' merchants, at 78 North Street, pictured in 1965. The blinds are down as this was a Sunday and the shop was closed. Shambles Alley (or The Crooked 'S') passes through the building between Clarks and Geering's shop at No 79.*

were previously part of Geerings and linked to their main shop at Nos 79 and 80 at first-floor level, across Shambles Alley. When he first moved, his advertisements showed that he was also a glass stockist but by the 1960s this wording had been dropped from the text, suggesting that he had surrendered glass sales to Smurthwaite's.In 1967 Clark's business was taken over by R. R. Perry and Sons who had shops in Bognor and Haywards Heath.[30] All the Clarks' staff stayed put so it was 'business as usual' but my father continued to refer to the shop as 'Clarks' though I am uncertain whether this was from force of habit or a form of protest. R. R. Perry closed the North Street shop in 1975 and moved to Adelaide Road after which the premises were taken over by Macari's famous coffee shop which, 35 years on, is still there – unlike, alas, the ironmongers and decorators' merchants described above.

Fig. 12. *The advertisement for William Clark & Sons which appeared in* The Martlet, *the magazine of Chichester High School for Boys, in 1953. This was the first one to give the new address, 78 North Street. At this time they were still a major stockist of window glass.*

PAINTS

PROTECTION and for DECORATION

WILLIAM

CLARK

& SONS

CROWN WALLPAPERS
ALL DECORATORS'
REQUIREMENTS

WINDOW GLASS
By the Crate or sold to Cut Sizes. A large selection of Obscure Glass in Stock.

Phone 2132

78, NORTH STREET, CHICHESTER

Phone 2132

---

[30] Clarks advertised in *The Martlet*, the magazine of Chichester High School for Boys, from 1951 and their last advertisement appeared in the Summer 1967 edition. Perrys did not continue the tradition.

```
................................19.

M.................................................

.................................................

Dr. to . . .

W. GREEN

——

Carpenter & Decorator

——

140 ORCHARD STREET, CHICHESTER, SUSSEX
```

The bill head of Wilfred Green, the author's father, who traded as carpenter and decorator in Chichester in the 1950s and 60s and had accounts with most of the businesses described in this article

Acknowledgements

In compiling this chapter I have received invaluable help from a number of people. I must start with Chichester District Museum, and Simon Kitchen in particular, who made available the museum's collection of photographs, ephemera and directories, and then the staff of West Sussex Record Office where the documentary searches were carried out. I was privileged to speak to many people who were associated with Jay's, Pine's and Smurthwaite's and shared their memories; Margaret Messam, Brian Clear, Vince Foote, Michael Timlick, Geoff Kent and Les Woods and I must thank Anne Scicluna who effected some of the introductions. Sincere thanks goes to Nick Brewer and Antony French of C. Brewer and Sons who supplied information about the last days of Smurthwaite's and provided the illustrations of the shop. Finally my thanks goes to Chichester Camera Club, and their chairman John Bradshaw, who kindly gave permission for the photographs of Pine's, Ray's and Clarks' shops to be published here. These photographs were taken by G Bevis, S Read and R Laing in 1965 as part of a club project recording the city's main streets. Finally I thank Andrew Berriman for seeking out the early William Clark advertisement in The Martlet.

8
FABRIC AND FURNISHINGS

SUSAN MILLARD

Wrap around you the drapery of your couch – and seek pleasant dreams
(Adapted from, William Cullen Bryant)

Fabric and furnishings: the things that people have in their homes, which express their personalities or their wealth and make them unique to themselves. This statement was as relevant in the distant past, when people began to fashion their own chairs and tables from local wood, or when the rich began to require wall hangings and bedcoverings, as it was in the nineteenth and twentieth centuries, when all towns and cities could boast a plethora of furniture and furnishing businesses catering for all tastes and pockets. Chichester was no exception and a study of the trades section of the street directories for the years 1886-1986 can reveal how the trade changed during this period. It also shows the close connections between fabric and furnishings, upholstery and furniture, and highlights the mystery of what exactly constitutes a 'draper'. Some draper's shops sold fabric for furnishings but others sold household linens or even clothing! Some sold both. There seems to be much overlap in all these areas.

In 1886 there were twenty-two businesses listed that advertised themselves as furnishers, furniture dealers, upholsterers, drapers or a mixture of the above. There was also Mrs Osborn of 48 North Street,[1] who described herself as a plumber and decorator. Two of the three 'furniture' businesses were also upholsterers and there were seven other upholsterers, or upholsteresses listed. Of the eleven 'drapers', some helpfully expanded on their description. For example Alfred Edwards of South Street was a 'Tailor & Draper', so he presumably concentrated on clothing rather than furnishings but George and H Penney of 18 North Street were 'Linen Drapers', so one could assume they were providing furnishings and household goods. However, over the years some of the terms used in the directories vary, so it can be difficult to tell whether a business changed its focus, or if it was the fashion at a particular date to be known as a 'General Draper', a 'Family Draper' or a 'Fancy Draper'.

---

[1] It should be mentioned that the numbering system in North Street was changed at the end of the nineteenth century. In 1886 the numbers ran south to north on the east side and then continued north to south along the west side. By 1900 they ran south to north on the west side and then north to south along the east side. So, a business that occupied the same premises in 1900 as it had in 1886 would be listed at a different number in the directories of those dates.

Of the furniture dealers, the one that prospered longest was John Leng and I shall deal with them in more detail later. Other furniture businesses that came and went during the period between 1886 and 1986 include Triggs, and Lewis & Co.

A. TRIGGS, house furnishing store, Eastgate Square, and later The Hornet

Triggs first appears in the 1914 directory as 'A Triggs, House Furnisher, 4 Eastgate'. By 1922 Alfred Triggs occupied nos 4, 5 and 6 Eastgate Square and by 1930 had expanded into no.7. In 1936 the Eastgate premises were demolished to make way for the Gaumont Cinema and by 1939 A Triggs was listed at The Hornet, and there was another advertisement for his son, Robert A Triggs, 'House Furnisher', at 20 North

Fig. 1. Triggs' imposing store at Eastgate Square on the site that became the Gaumont cinema and later the swimming pool

Fig. 2. Lewis & Co. at the Old Theatre South Street

Pallant. Over the next few years R A Triggs was listed as 'Furniture Dealer' and then as 'R A Triggs (Sussex) Ltd, House Furnishers and Carpet Suppliers', last appearing in the directories in 1971.

LEWIS & CO. house furnishers, 27-30 Southgate

Lewis & Co appear in the same directories as Triggs. They were one of the multiple trade businesses that

were common in the first half of the 20th century. They advertised themselves as 'Lewis & Co, Complete House Furnishers, Upholsterers & Cabinet makers, Removal Contractors and Warehousemen, 27, 28, 30 and 30a Southgate'. They acquired a garage and store in Lyndhurst Road and Caledonian Road and by 1939 they were also advertising 'A large selection of seasonable fabrics always in stock. Curtains and loose covers a speciality. Funeral Furnishers. Also at Bognor Regis'. However, by 1971 the advertisement was reduced to 'Lewis & Co, House furnishers, Southgate'. In 1974 there was an advertisement for 'Lewis of Chichester, Furniture Removal Contractors, Lion Street' but by the 1980s there was no trace.

Fig. 3. Lewis & Co. on the west side of Southgate

There were numerous upholstery firms listed in the Pike's Directory and many more started up, only to disappear again during the first half of the twentieth century. One business that was listed in 1886 and was continued by members of the same family until at least 1954, is Wimhurst's upholsterers. In 1886 Alfred Wimhurst was listed as an upholsterer at 64 North Street and by 1900 he was listed as 'Cabinet Maker and Upholsterer, 30 North Street'. By 1922 Mrs Wimhurst was listed as the proprietor and 'undertaker' has been added to the description. G A Wimhurst (probably Alfred's son George) was listed in 1933 at St Martin's Square as well as 29 North Street. The description now included furniture repair and boasts a 'Motor Hearse'! Finally, in 1950 and 1954 Harry A F Wimhurst (George's younger brother) was running the business, first at St Martin's Square and, finally, at 20 Franklin Place.

Another name that appears in a number of the directories, albeit with many twists and turns along the way, was Turner. In 1886 T Turner, upholsterer was listed at 42 North Street. By 1900 there were two Turners listed; Tom Turner, furniture dealer, 62 North Street; and John Turner who was running an unlikely business combination of 'Beer Retailer and Furniture Dealer' at 2 & 3 St Pancras! He was listed again in 1903 simply as a Furniture Dealer at 7 St Pancras, but disappears thereafter. T Turner, furniture dealer of 62 North Street reappears in 1909 but by 1922 it was 'B C Turner, Furniture and Wardrobe Dealer, 131 St Pancras'. In 1933 Turner & Bushell, furniture dealers were listed at 2A Little London with Arthur Turner, upholsterer also at Little London. By 1954 Turner & Bushell were no longer in the directory but Arthur, the upholsterer had moved to the rear of 93 The Hornet, via a spell at 3 Lion Street. He was not listed after 1954. It is not certain that any of these Turners were related but given the proximity of some of the addresses and similarity between the trades, some connection seems likely. An upholstery firm that was established in the middle of the twentieth century, after buying the 'goodwill' of an earlier business, was 'The Practical Upholsters' and I shall consider them in the case studies.

There were several firms of drapers that appeared in 1886 and survive right through to the middle of the twentieth century. Sykes and Penney's were listed until 1974. As mentioned earlier, George and Harry Penney were listed as linen drapers at 18 North Street. By 1914 they were listed as 'H Penney & Co, General Drapers, 73 North Street'. By 1950 the description was expanded to 'Drapers, Ladies' Outfitters, Milliners and Household Textiles' but by 1968 they were described as fabric dealers and had moved to 60 East Street and, finally, in 1974 they were listed as soft furnishers'.

Sykes first appear as 'Turnbull & Sykes, Drapers and Silk Merchants, 9 & 10 South Street'. By 1922 the business had the familiar title of Alfred Sykes & Son and the description included millinery for which Sykes was to become well known. For some years the description also included 'Ladies Outfitters etc' but by 1974 it was 'Drapers and Milliners, fabrics etc.'. The business eventually moved out of the centre of Chichester and continued in St Pancras for a number of years. Charge & Co., although listed as drapers, always showed a leaning towards clothing rather than furnishings. The person who composed their advertisement in the 1886 directory had a poetic turn of phrase. As well as drapers they were described as 'Hosiers & Haberdashers, Flowers & Feathers, Millinery & Mantles'! They were listed at a variety of addresses in South Street and the description changed over the years: in 1933, as well as drapers they were described as blouse specialists. However, by 1968 they had dropped the drapers listing and were simply 'Ladies and Children's Outfitters'. Doman's appear in the directory until 1971 but they will be dealt with later.

Henry Denyer, draper of 84 North Street was listed from 1900 to 1954 and Christopher Doman recalls that Mr Denyer 'was a lovely smiley friendly man'. George Edward Lever (later G Lever & Son), of 28 East Street was listed from 1903 to 1950. Geerings first appeared in the 1909 Directory at 78 North Street and, although described as drapers or a drapery store, until 1950, they always include millinery in their advertisements. By 1974 they were described as a department store.

LENG'S furniture emporium, Eastgate Square/St Pancras

The 1886 Pike's directory entry for John Leng's shop at Eastgate must be one of the longest and diverse in that volume! The advertisement listed numerous trades and types of work undertaken by the family firm, proclaiming 'John Leng Furniture and Carpet Warehouse, Cabinet Maker, Broker and Undertaker, Upholsterer and

Paperhanging, Appraiser and House Agent. A large stock of Antique and modern furniture'. By the time this remarkable advertisement was in print the business was already well established in Chichester. John Leng came to Chichester from Yorkshire and in circa 1811 set up in business at Northgate. He was, primarily, a machine maker and it is possible that he came south at the time of the Luddite uprisings in the north. In a deed of 5 September he is described as having recently purchased a piece of land at Northgate, his occupation a thrashing machine maker. He continued his trade making agricultural machinery in his workshop, but he also had an interest in carpentry and house furnishings and it was this side of the business that is remembered by so many people and which was to survive well into the 20th century. He married Ann Lambert, a Chichester girl and they had several children including John, born 1813 and William, born 1816. In 1829 John Leng senior died, leaving a widow and five children, and as John Leng junior was only fifteen his uncle, Israel Leng, came down from Yorkshire to help run the business. There could be many reasons why, at this time, they decided to concentrate on the furniture side of the business (possibly they now had to contend with the Swing Riots and machine breaking in the South!). We can only speculate. A set of three business cards, with forty years between each and dated 1865, 1905 and 1945, all claim the business was established in 1824. It is not clear at what date the business first occupied the property that still survives between St Paul's churchyard and The Bell Inn (1a Broyle Road), but we do know that it survived the 1960s demolition of the old Somerstown and, later, the construction of the ring road. For many years it housed Mazzones's sweetshop, which is still remembered with affection by many Cicestrian's.

Three years after his father died John junior became a committed Christian. He was, initially, involved with the Congregationalists and later became a travelling preacher for the Bible Christian Church. This was a Methodist denomination which had been founded in 1815 in the West Country by William O'Bryan, a Wesleyan Methodist preacher. While John was away preaching the business seems to have been in good hands, as it continued to grow under the management of Israel and John's brother William. In 1838 another property - at Eastgate - was acquired and when John gave up preaching in 1843 the business was then operating from two premises.

John and William continued to work successfully together with other members of the family and in the 1870s the Leng identity was firmly established when the 'new' Eastgate shop front was fitted out as a larger replica of the original Northgate property. At around the same time, in 1874, the business was divided, John taking the Eastgate shop and William continuing at Northgate.

However, the Northgate business only occasionally advertised in the local directories and in 1902 it was finally wound up, a year after William died, aged 85. Meanwhile, the Eastgate business went from strength to strength. Throughout his life John Leng had continued his interest and commitment to the non-conformist cause and in 1893 he secured the use of a chapel at Fisher, in South Mundham. Unfortunately, it was struck by lightning and caught fire but John Leng was persistent and in 1896 bought the site. A new Zion chapel was built in 1905, just a few years before he died, aged 94, in 1908. After his death the business passed to his three sons, Alfred, Charles and Ebenezer.

Between 1900 and 1914 the business continued to be advertised as 'John Leng & sons, Cabinet Maker & Upholsterer, 1& 156 St Pancras'. However, after the First World War ended in 1918, there was an increasing demand for new furniture and furnishings and the department store began to make an appearance. Leng's took advantage of this trend and expanded the furnishing side. They seem to have resurrected the old 1886 advertisement and brought it up to date as the 1922 Kelly's entry reads 'John Leng & Sons, Complete House Furnishers, Cabinet Makers and Upholsterers, Paperhangers & House Agents. A good selection of carpets, floor cloth, linoleum, matting etc.'. Charles died in 1924 and an advertisement for the same year shows Alfred and Ebenezer as the partners. Alfred was listed as an Alderman in the 1927 directory but he died in 1933 aged 81. His brother Ebenezer died in 1942 aged 85.

A good set of account books, day books and ledgers survive for 1837-1950, which provide a unique insight into the type of goods sold and the variety of customers served throughout most of the period of the firm's existence. The huge range of services offered by Leng's in their 1886 advertisement included 'undertaker'. The close working relationship between cabinet makers, upholsterers and funeral directors is in evidence here, as the firm certainly supplied coffins, and funerals, to some of the most well-known families in Chichester. In 1854 the customer's account book records an entry on 28 October, 'Mr Budden of East Street paid 16 shillings for a coffin for E C Budden'. And on 20th November 1864 the supply of a coffin, the use of the pall and attendance, and the hire of hatbands and four bearers, cost Mr Ballard £2. 19s. 1d. After the end of the 19th century this was a service that was becoming more specialised and it seems to have been dropped by Leng's, perhaps to concentrate on the furniture and furnishing side of the business. In 1922 upholstery was still offered and this would have included the making of mattresses. In February 1927 the customer's account book records that Mrs George Ballard was charged 15 shillings and 6 pence for 'carding and making a 4ft 6 in. mattress, 4lbs wool added.' It also records that the bill was not settled until May 1928. Perhaps Mrs Ballard wanted to be sure that she was entirely satisfied with the product, as the same lady had earlier returned a hip bath!

Many of Leng's customers were other Chichester shop owners. In October 1917 Mr Bastow of North Street ordered 16-and-1/8th sq. yds of lino and a hearth rug, which cost a total of £3. 18s. 11d. This included the 5s. 3d. that it cost to fit and lay the lino. Other local business names that appear are Penney, Halsted, Clark, Shippam, Wyatt and Wingham. Various educational establishments were also buying from them including Westhampnett School, Oliver Whitby School and Bishop Otter College. Also on the books were the Matron of the Infirmary, The High Sheriff, Canon Deane, and Lady Milbank.

Fig. 4. Site of Leng's, adjacent to St Pancras Church

It is interesting that the two World Wars appear to have had very little effect on the day to day running of the business. The Home Front appears to have required the same services as in peacetime but, of course, there is nothing in the surviving records of the business to indicate the likely reduction in personnel and increase in women workers! The Second World War makes a brief impact on the business, as the day book for September 1939 shows. Throughout September and into October 1939 there was a flurry of orders for gas masks and, curiously, gas mask cases. The first entry on September 8th reads 'received 6 shillings for 5 gas mask cases'. The orders for cases continue until the 11th when the entries begin to record 'gas masks'. Perhaps the cases arrived first to be followed by the masks themselves? The customer's account book for the same month records the possible fitting of black-out blinds for Arnold Cooper and Tompkins of East Street, as they were charged 11 shillings for 'cutting out two black linen blinds and fixing up rollers at entrance doors to office.

The type of work undertaken continued to be wide-ranging. On 18 July 1939 for the cost of 2 shillings they repaired an old Windsor chair and treated it for worms for Mrs Donaldson of Selsey. But on 13 April 1943, at the other end of the scale, they provided a customer in Sloane Square with furniture to the value of £603 and 7 shillings, the bill being paid promptly on 23 April. The furniture supplied included wardrobes, mattresses and bedsteads, writing tables, card tables, chests of drawers, dining table and chairs, bookcase, tallboy, dinner wagons, a dressing glass and sideboard and a loo table (used for the card game lanterloo).

The last surviving ledger ends in 1950 and a blank 1950s statement is attached to the inside front cover, which lists the directors as H J Hill, H J K Hill, A H Hill, G Hill, M A Hill. Another business card has J M Hill added, hand-written, to the list. The Hills were all direct descendants of the original John Leng. John junior's daughter Harriet married William Hill, a Bible Christian minister. Although born in Devon, William was recorded on the 1881 census living in Ventnor on the Isle of Wight.

William and Harriet Hill had several children and their son, Harold John, inherited the business. Harold John's name, together with his sons, Harold John Kenrick and Alec Herman were still listed on the business stationary at the time it was sold. Of the others listed at that time; M A Hill and J M Hill were probably Harold John Kendrick's children. He married Gladys Carver in 1927 and their children Muriel A and John M were born in 1928 and 1938, respectively.

So, John Leng & Sons continued to be run by members of the same family right up until the business was sold in 1965. In all, six generations. Some time after the business was sold, the Eastgate building was demolished and replaced by a new one, which for some years housed the St Wilfrid's Hospice shop. At present it is occupied by Cloth Kits. However, the Northgate building, where it all started, still survives.

DOMAN'S, drapers, 76 East Street

Fig. 5. Doman's East Street store before WW II

William Doman was born in 1836 in Basingstoke, Hampshire but moved to Middlesex to learn the drapery trade. By 1868 he had moved to Chichester and established his own drapery business at 76 East Street. He married Alice Ellen Heath in 1869 and they had several children. Their son, William Heath Doman, followed his father into the business and in 1890 opened a second shop at 24 North Street. In 1899 he married Maud Alice Vick, whose family lived in Tower Street. By 1914 the business had expanded and the East Street shop was now advertised as 'William Doman, Drapers' whilst 24 North Street was advertised as 'William Doman, Drapers & Outfitters'. William Heath Doman and Maud Alice had a daughter (Barbara Maude) and three sons. One of the sons, William Frederick Hugh, died young but Denzil Robert and Arthur Cedric both joined the business. Both shops traded as 'Doman and Son' but kept their separate status. The East Street shop continued with the drapery department, selling fabrics, sheets, blankets and towels and from 1920 was run by Denzil Robert (known as Dickie). The North Street shop housed the lingerie side of the business and continued to be run by William until his younger son, Arthur, joined the firm.

Both brothers married, Arthur to Betty Murray and Dickie to Mary Bastow, whose family owned the Bastow chemist's shop in Chichester. Dickie and Mary had two sons, Christopher William, born in 1937 and Richard Hugh, born in 1941.

William Heath Doman died in 1948 and brothers, Dickie and Arthur ran the two branches as partners. After about four years they decided to split the company, which allowed them more scope to develop their individual sides of the business. Arthur continued with the North Street shop, specialising in ladies' fashions. Kelly's Directory for 1950 shows the East Street shop continuing to be listed as 'Doman & Son, Drapers'. But the North Street shop was now listed as 'Doman & Son, Ladies Outfitters and Costumiers' (for further details see chapter on Personal Attire).

Dickie continued to develop the drapery shop in East Street, specialising in linens and soft furnishings, now known as 'Doman's Furnishings'. He was keen to gain a reputation for quality work and an advertisement in the *Chichester Observer* in March 1950 proclaims 'Domans of Chichester, loose covers and curtains made by experts'. Christopher Doman describes the old East Street shop as a 'funny little place'. He recalls that 'people used to come from a long way away to have curtains made by that funny little place in Chichester! It really was, it was quite extraordinary.'

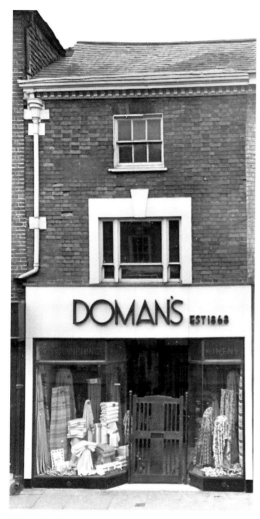

Fig. 6. The Doman store in East Street after the refurbishment in c. 1960

Christopher also remembers an incident when in about 1959 Barclay's bank was rebuilt. When the strong rooms, which were below street level, were excavated Doman's, which was next door, had to be propped up. Christopher recalls that his father took his younger son, Richard, down to the station to put him on the train to Bournemouth, where he was going to spend a year in training at a big store there. 'It turned out that Doman's had an Elizabethan rubble wall! Father came back to find that the wall had collapsed and at the top of the house were half a dozen workroom girls with heavy sewing machines and bales of cloth in an unstable building. He got them all down one by one'. After this incident it was necessary to demolish the building and build a new one, so for about a year

Doman's Furnishings Ltd carried on business in what is now Pizza Express in South Street. When the new East Street building was finally completed it extended over two floors and also included a basement. It was considered to be very fine and modern.

The basement housed the linens and the furnishing fabrics, and the offices and workrooms were on the other two floors. Christopher also remembers that 'from the top of the lift shaft there was the best view of Chichester cathedral. You could get out onto the roof and there was the cathedral, a wonderful view!'

The new shop heralded a period of expansion for Doman's. Dickie's son Richard came into the business in 1959 and the business continued to grow throughout the 1960s. By 1968 Dickie managed to acquire what was the Scotch Wool Shop, next door at 77 East Street, which provided even more space for the business to develop. By this time the business concentrated on specialist furnishing fabrics, curtains and loose covers and was advertised as 'Doman's Furnishings Ltd, Household Linens (soft furnishing specialists)'. They prided themselves on their wide choice of furnishing fabrics and employed over 60 staff. They also acquired H. E. Foyster Ltd, a reproduction furniture shop, which was at 36 East Street, on the corner of Little London. There was also a subsidiary business in Stirling Road.

The main business premises continued to be at 76 East Street and in 1968 Doman's was able to celebrate their centenary in the same building where William Doman had set up his drapery business one hundred years before! There was a full page spread in the *Chichester Observer* to celebrate the event. However, in 1974 the old premises at 76 East Street, together with the former Scotch Wool Shop building, was sold and the fabrics and linens business soon moved to purpose-built premises in The Hornet. But the Hornet shop closed in 1980 along with the rest of the old Doman Empire and the building was, for many years, occupied by a motor factors firm. Now, ironically, it houses another furnishing business, Countrystyle Interiors.

However, although the old Doman's was no longer a familiar sight in the city, in 1984 Richard Doman started a separate business in Stirling Road, 'Richard Doman Furnishing'. In July 1985 an advertisement in the Chichester Festivities Programme claimed that his 25 years experience in soft furnishings ranged from 'the installation of the John Piper Tapestries in Chichester Cathedral to the carpeting of a Mosque in Riyadh'. The Stirling Road site at Forum House is still occupied by Richard Doman's furnishing business., so, although not with the same company, Richard is the fourth generation of the Doman family to run a fabric and furnishings business in Chichester.

Conclusion

This chapter has been concerned with fabric and furnishing businesses and concentrated on the furniture, upholstery and drapery trades. However, as has been shown 'drapery' can encompass various branches of the clothing business as well as house furnishings.

Furniture and furnishing businesses can include the buying and selling of furniture and furnishings, cabinet making, upholstery and even funeral services.

Other trades that help make a house a home were often under the umbrella of 'Complete Furniture' businesses. For example, not only linoleum and carpet-fitting but also carpentry and paperhanging were often included. However, by 1933 the *Chichester Observer* was carrying many more advertisements for these trades as separate businesses. Homes also require entertainment 'furnishings' and in the first half of the 20th century there continued to be many advertisements for businesses selling and tuning pianos. However, by 1953 the majority of advertisements for home entertainment were for televisions and radios.

It would seem that most furnishing businesses expanded or contracted according to their own endeavours, the economic climate, or the fashion of the day. For example, pre 1950 linoleum was an important feature in every home but after 1950 carpets were considered more desirable by a wider section of society. The businesses survived or profited, in some cases, by offering a wider range of services or, in others, specialisation. Also, different generations have their own individual ideas of how a business should be run. Sometimes a business closed because there was nobody in the next generation able, or willing, to take it on. However, although many of the furnishing businesses that were situated in the city centre in 1950 no longer exist in the same place, or in the same form, pockets of survival can still be found in the environs - and astonishingly successful businesses as well. Comment on two is given in the Coda below.

CODA: THE PRACTICAL UPHOLSTERERS
– (a peripatetic business!)

Harold Pullen was born in 1914 at East Ashling, near Chichester. He trained in the furniture and upholstery trade in Chichester and in 1952, together with Horace Lambourne, set up The Practical Upholsterers Ltd.

Just after the Second World War Harold and Horace were both working for Cuddington's of 77 St Pancras. Cuddington's sold house furnishings (including loose covers for upholstered furniture), bedroom and three-piece suites and lino etc., and they first appear in the Chichester trade directories in 1933. In 1937 they advertised in a programme for 'The Rebel Maid' performed at the Assembly Rooms '...ask all your friends where they go for furniture of

Fig. 7. Harold Pullen

quality....at lowest possible prices'. Cuddington's were also agents for Marmet baby carriages and eventually decided to concentrate on the baby carriage trade. Harold Pullen and Horace Lambourne bought the 'goodwill' of the furnishing side of the business and started out as The Practical Upholsterers. Their first premises were a shed in Farr's Yard in South Pallant and at this time they were known as The Practical Upholsterer's Farrs Ltd. But they soon took over the top floor of the building and an advertisement in the *Chichester Observer* for 7 March 1953 gives the address as 10 South Pallant. The advertisement reads 'Mattresses cleaned & remade in same or new cases, Spring Interiors a speciality'. Mattresses were remade by pulling out all the old horse hair and putting it through a carding machine to untangle and clean it. This could be an incredibly dusty job! The new or cleaned mattress case (usually of black and white hair-proof ticking) was then re-stuffed using the refreshed horsehair. Sometimes extra hair had to be added. They were then stitched round the side and tufted through the top. The best quality mattresses were made from the hair from white horses, which was soft but resilient. This process was also used for re-upholstering furniture.

When Jen Wingham, Harold Pullen's niece, joined the firm in 1957 the workforce consisted of Mr Pullen, Mr Lambourne, Pat Lambourne (Horace's daughter) and Jen, plus about five other members of staff. The work they undertook was primarily upholstery, carpets and curtains. At that time carpeting was only available in 27 or 36 inch widths so, if a larger carpet was required, they were hand-sewn together using a special frame set up in the workshop from which the carpets could be suspended. Eventually, Harold Pullen bought out Horace Lambourne.

In 1958 they moved to 12a St Martin's Square behind Wyatt's salerooms. They occupied an old sail maker's loft, which had originally been stables. Harold's son Graham joined the firm in 1962 to learn all aspects of upholstery and furniture making as well as carpet fitting. In 1971 Kevin Lawrence was taken on as apprentice upholsterer, learning his trade from Tom Miller, who had once been employed by Maples, the most respected upholstery firm in London. Whilst working for Maples Tom upholstered the green leather seating in the House of Commons. During their time in St Martin's Square the business grew rapidly and at one time 13 members of staff were employed there. The old loft in St Martin's Square was in a wonderful old building and an interesting place in which to work, but getting the furniture up to the top floor could cause problems. It often had to be hauled up to the fire escape platform on ropes!

Kevin Lawrence tells a story of how he and one of the other apprentices were always playing tricks on one another and on one memorable occasion he poured water from the top window down on to what he thought was the other apprentice coming out of the toilet below but, in fact, it was the owner of the next door catering firm coming out with a pile of crockery! Fortunately, despite the soaking, he managed to hang on to all the plates, cups, and saucers and nothing was broken.

The business developed a good reputation for quality work and built up a core of customers who had not only local properties but also London homes. Much of their work involved trips to the capital and the Home Counties. No job was too small though and they were also quite happy to mend a broken spring or make curtains and lay carpets for the smallest property.

Harold Pullen retired in 1990 but the business was carried on by his son, Graham and niece Jen. Kevin Lawrence was taken on as a Director in 1987. They stayed in St Martin's Square until 1991 when the owner of the building sold to a developer and they had to find another property to rent. They decided it would be more cost effective to move out of Chichester and found a unit at Walberton. They carried on the business there until 1997, when they bought a former builder's yard in Pound Farm Road and were able to move back to the city environs. At this time, as well as three directors they also employed Graham's wife Caroline and her cousin Paul Ayling, together with several other members of staff. In recent years Graham's son, Stephen, has followed in his father and grandfather's footsteps in learning all aspects of the trade.

A true family firm, it is nearly sixty years since they started out in South Pallant. They are still working from the premises in Pound Farm Road, but as the current generation nears and passes retirement age it is unlikely that Stephen Pullen will be able to carry it on in the same form. Quality furnishing is a very labour intensive trade but overheads are high, and, in today's throwaway society, furniture is cheap to replace. There will always be some quality work required but the days of city centre firms who can afford to employ staff are certainly numbered.

I would like to thank Ron Iden for his invaluable assistance, in particular for resolving issues with the Leng family tree. Also grateful thanks go to Christopher Doman and Jennifer Wingham for readily giving me their time and allowing me to interview them. Thanks also to Richard Doman and Kevin Lawrence. Lastly, I wish to record the business of Whitmore Jones in Oving Road. The firm was founded in 1909 by Arthur Whitmore Jones in Albert Road, Southsea; late in the 1930s he bought a second shop in Cosham, and straight after WW II (in 1946) a third shop - the present premises in Oving Road. Arthur was the grandfather of the present proprietor (Chris Whitmore Jones) and must at the time have felt huge satisfaction with what he may have seen as his life's work - the provision of an independent business for each of his three sons.

It seems likely that the present firm may claim to be Chichester's longest-established business to be continuously owned by the same family throughout its 102 years of trading. That is an achievement of considerable merit and one that, despite the imminent arrival in Chichester of a John Lewis store, Chris is planning to continue. As he said recently, the firm has withstood a number of considerable shocks across its long history - and has no intention of succumbing now. Bravo!

Sources (all at WSRO): Add Ms 11,459 (Title deed); Add Mss 18,212-12,230 (Leng's records); AM 313/1 (Bill heads); Cutten Mss D/2/9 (Newspaper cutting of article by Bernard Price); Par 44/9/3 (Receipts); MP 1427 (Reminiscence); MP 1966 (Adult Education study); PM 401 (GOAD Maps)

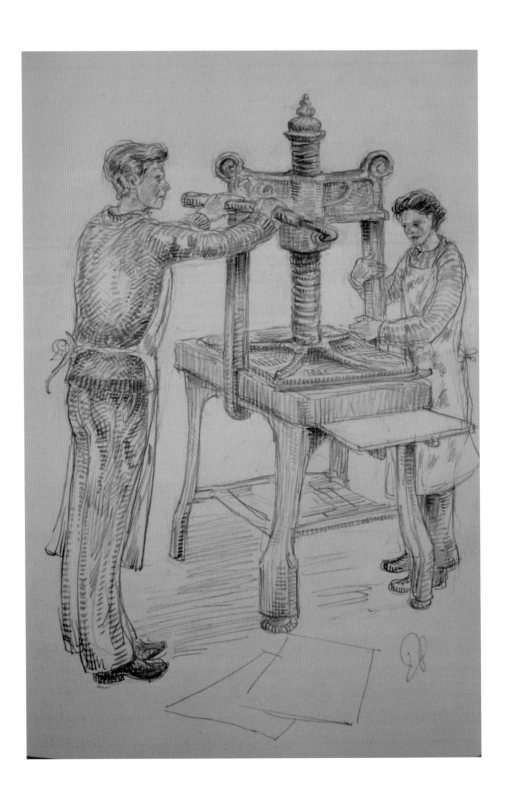

9

PAPER AND PRINT

STEPHEN PRICE

'Tis the good reader makes the good book
(Emerson)

The printed word lies at the very heart of our day-to-day lives; it is central to our community and to ourselves as individuals. Over the years we have taken for granted the ability to go in to town and buy, for example, a novel, order some programmes for our school show or perhaps pick up our specially printed wedding invitations. The businesses who provide us with these services help us to do what we do and be who we are, though I'm sure the tradesmen involved don't see their roles in quite such an elevated light. It is an area of business that goes back centuries but also one that has been revolutionized in recent decades.

Supermarkets dominate most people's weekly spending and this is reflected in our changing shopping habits for books and stationery. Publishers chase market-share by giving these behemoths discounts of a size independent retailers can only dream of so that we can buy bestsellers with our groceries. Today the independent bookshop is under pressure to survive like never before and there is just one specialist national bookshop chain. It is another example of the inexorable creep towards homogenization of the High Street.

Perhaps most significantly the personal computer, digitalization and the internet have had profound affects on those involved in the paper and print business. For the bookseller the challenge is that new books can be ordered online and delivered next day to our homes, and even second-hand and collectible books can be 'discovered' and sourced from all round the world. Books lend themselves to online business particularly well as they don't perish, are easily packed and, unlike clothing, the only question of fitting is whether or not you can squeeze the volume on to your shelves. Print businesses are not immune to these changes either as now we can so often design and print paper material at home, perhaps not always perfectly, but well enough to satisfy our needs. What follows is not a comprehensive or exhaustive study of all the booksellers and printers who have been based in Chichester over the last fifty years or so, but is instead a look at half a dozen firms who pursued these areas of trade and are remembered by Cicestrians with interest and affection.

W.H. BARRETT, 1 South Street

Barrett's was a fixture in Chichester for many years. In recent times a number of national bookshop chains have attempted to position themselves as being at the heart of the local community but I imagine that is something Barrett's never had to trouble themselves with. Situated at 1, South Street (also identified as 2, South Street, before the site was re-numbered in the nineteenth century), their location was such that they couldn't have been more central and in advertisements they sometimes gave their address simply as 'The Cross'. The business was started in the 1870s by William Henry Barrett and traded until the mid-1950s. The shop offered customers a range of products and services with the emphasis on being a bookseller, stationer and newsagent.

Fig. 1. Barrett's 'dressed' for the Queen's coronation in 1953

However they also sold art materials, Goss China, fancy leather goods, ran a subscription and circulating library and were printers. An example of the print work is described in The Mitford Archive which lists 'an account of the proceedings relating to the Election of a Member of Parliament for the Borough of Midhurst, January & February 1874 ... compiled and published by W. H. Barrett (Chichester, 1874)'.

For someone looking at early photographs of Chichester Barrett's is a recurring feature. Naturally, many images of the City are of the Cross looking toward West Street and the Cathedral, so this shop on the corner of West Street and South Street is often included. In his trilogy of Chichester books, Bernard Price includes pictures that capture the changing times well and serve to show the longevity of the Barrett's business. We can see sheep making their way round the Cross in the late nineteenth century, a crowd gathered as King George V is proclaimed, and later the shop again as a throng forms on V.E. Day, 8 May 1945. Through it all W.H. Barrett was a constant. The location of the shop is interesting too as the site has been traded on for centuries and in one of those curious echoes of land usage that history sometimes reveals previous traders have included booksellers and stationers, Glover's prior to Barrett's and William Smithers before that.

THE WESSEX BOOKSHOP, 24 South Street

More recently, the 'Wessex' will be remembered by many. Situated at 24 South Street, it was the main independent bookseller of new books for the town. It was owned by husband and wife, John and Charmian Ball, but managed by Elizabeth Allen. Miss Allen had learnt her trade with Hatchard's in London and, with the owners, presided over this general bookshop from the mid-1960s through to the early 1980s. To begin with Miss Allen lived in the flat over the shop but in later years the space was used by a gallery business, with access provided through the bookshop. When the Wessex closed there remained a bookshop at the address, first Hudson's and then a branch of the erstwhile national chain Dillons, before that too closed in the early 1990s. The Wessex was a relatively small shop and it was Dillons who expanded the premises, eating into the site's garden space at the rear. Miss Allen worked at the address throughout these changes of ownership but left Dillons and ended her bookselling career with Hammick's Bookshop at 65 East Street.

Fig. 2. The attractive frontage of the 'Wessex'

For a large portion of the post-war years Chichester was fortunate to be served by two really excellent second-hand bookshops where book-lovers could browse and talk, buy what they had gone in for but also pick-up that volume that perhaps they didn't even know had existed when they had first entered. It was a time when booksellers worked by booklists rather than computers; a time when stock, book knowledge, and service were key. Offord and Meynell was the first of the two shops to open and then, later, the Chichester Bookshop started trading. There is a sense beyond nostalgia or simple sentimentality that says good second-hand and antiquarian bookshops and a market town, indeed a Cathedral City, seem a good compliment to each other, a comfortable fit.

CHICHESTER BOOKSHOP, 39 Southgate

Throughout most of the period The Wessex Bookshop was trading, you could have turned right out of their door, clutching your new book, and strolled down South Street in search of an old volume at the Chichester Bookshop. This was owned by

George Thompson and was opened in mid-1967 at 39 Southgate where he was joined in 1968 by John Dent. Mr. Dent had learnt his bookselling profession in Brighton and it was he, as Manager, who became the face familiar to customers while Mr Thompson involved himself more with house visits or auction-going in the search for good stock. The premises was a narrow building and, whilst the shop traded on just two floors, because of some steps and a split-level ground floor, it had the feeling of being bigger than it perhaps really was. It could be characterized as a general

Fig.3. George Thompson at 39 Southgate

bookshop with an antiquarian section and like all good shops of this sort could surprise with a rare volume or an item of ephemera. It was an environment where the interests of customers became known and pleasure could be taken from drawing a volume to the attention of one of the regulars.

In the early 1970s John Dent became a Partner in the business and the shop became Chichester Bookshop Ltd. For a period in the 1980s they also had a second shop - at 33 Southgate. This building

Fig. 4. John Dent 1996

was of interest as it still had the wheel and hoist from when the property had been used by a corn merchant. It was here that the business kept the more collectible or antiquarian volumes, while the shop at 39 Southgate sold the more general stock. This venture lasted for just a few years before the business returned to being housed solely at its original premises.

George Thompson died in 1989 and Mr. Dent took the business over in May 1994 running it until May 1997 as John Dent's Bookshop. Upon his retirement, the business was sold to Nick Howell and the shop once again traded as the Chichester Bookshop. Mr Howell subsequently

Fig. 5. Sheila Holden, Senior Assistant   sold to Chris and Carol Lowndes who took the shop through to forty years of trading before it closed in the summer of 2008.

OFFORD & MEYNELL, 50 East Street

About forty years was also the length of time that Offord and Meynell Ltd traded, opening in the summer of 1946 at 50 East Street and closing, then as Meynell's Bookshop, in the autumn of 1985. Charles Offord and Viv Meynell had become friends during the Second World War and when they left the army they became business partners deciding to open a bookshop. After about four years Charles Offord went his own way, becoming a farmer, and Mr. Meynell remained to continue with the business. To work with the written word was a natural choice for Mr. Meynell coming from a distinguished literary and artistic family. His grandparents included the author, editor and publisher Wilfrid Meynell and the poet, critic and essayist Alice Meynell. His father was the author, Everard Meynell, and his uncle, Sir Francis Meynell, founded the Nonesuch Press.

Fig. 6. Viv Meynell

It was particularly during these early years of trade that Mr Meynell sought to supplement the takings from the books by selling watercolours and prints at the shop. For six years he also worked as a reporter for the *West Sussex Gazette* & *South of England Advertiser* writing, often in the basement of the shop, about various Chichester events. He then became Superintendent Registrar based at Theatre Lane and this, combined with the search for stock, inevitably led to time away from the business. During these periods his wife Patsy would run the shop, supposedly part-time, but of course the hours over-ran and her involvement was integral to the day to day running. Her popularity with the customers was no doubt heightened by her homemade biscuits and flapjacks which were sold alongside the coffee.

Fig. 7. The former frontage at 50 East Street, now completely replaced by the current occupant, New Look

Fig. 8. The coffee bar at Offord & Meynell - a considerable innovation in its time

It almost feels a slight on Mr. Meynell's bookselling skills and experience to say it, but when talking to Cicestrians about the shop for this chapter, it quickly became apparent that what people particularly remember was the coffee. Coffee and books go undeniably well together and, today, to find a coffee shop in a bookstore is common but it most certainly wasn't in 1954 when Mr. Meynell's coffee bar was put in place. In fact this was a real innovation in bookselling. I well remember being taken to the shop as a boy and being aware, even at that young age, of the coffee bar giving an air of easy sophistication. A delightful sign, written by Sir Francis Meynell, advertised the drinks that were available and, in retrospect, also highlighted what was then the unusual nature of what was on offer:

Coffee made in the Italian 'Espresso' machine is the cream of coffee, elixir of coffee. Sevenpence for a small cup served black ('espresso nero') in the true Italian fashion: for Admirals, nay for Bishops. Or eightpence with milk (capucino) [sic]: *for Captains of Industry & their Ladies. Black or white, an Espresso will delight all coffee-minded Cicestrians.*

An area at the back of the shop was given over to coffee drinking, not a large area, with sofas and chairs that can engulf you, as you might experience today, but simply a bar and some stools to sit on. Surrounded by volumes, the coffee was good and conversation encouraged, but the focus remained the books. Customers came for refreshment, sometimes these were people who wouldn't ordinarily have ventured into a bookshop, and they would drink and notice the stock and perhaps make purchases. The enterprise was a success and helped put the business firmly on the town map.

The shop was visited by many eminent figures from the theatrical and literary worlds. Graham Greene was a customer as was Laurie Lee; Jon Stallworthy, Ted Walker, George Macbeth and others gave poetry readings, and on these occasions new books would be sold. This continued for thirty years until 1976, when increases in overheads became too much for a second-hand bookshop to sustain, and Mr. Meynell moved his business to 11, The Hornet. The shop, now simply called Meynell's Bookshop, was upstairs and less centrally located than the East Street site, but enough customers followed the business for it to trade for nearly a further decade before closing in 1985. Its closure was a sad loss to the Chichester retail and cultural scene.

MOORE & TILLYER, 39 East Street

Throughout the period Offord and Meynell traded, a little further up the road at 39 East Street was Moore & Tillyer Ltd. This is a business that continues to trade today, now based in Metro House at Northgate, but the premises that were familiar to so many - the stationery shop in East Street and the print works in St John's Street - have gone.

The business was founded by John William Moore in mid-Victorian times and was originally based in Eastgate Square but moved to 39 East Street, opposite the Corn

Fig. 9. Moore and Tillyer, .c. 1995

Exchange, at the beginning of the 1880s. Here Moore's business as printer, publisher and stationer became established in Chichester life. All types of printing were done at this East Street address, from commonplace work demanded by private and business customers, to the more ambitious publication of the Chichester Directory, Handbook and Almanac the earliest of which I have seen being printed by J.W. Moore in 1871. At the time the Chichester Directory was an invaluable way for businesses to promote themselves and their services to potential customers, but now it has become an indispensable tool for local historians seeking an understanding of commercial life in a particular year.

Each month J. W. Moore also published *The Chichester 'ABC' Railway Guide* and in the 1890 Chichester Directory this *Guide* is described as 'Showing at a glance how and when to go from Chichester to any Railway Station on the London, Brighton and South Coast Line, and also the Principal Railway Stations in the South of England: Together with a Table of Fares, Postal Regulations, List of Carriers, &c., &c.' All this could be had for one penny.

Before the first decade of the twentieth century had passed, the business had grown and the print-side of the company had moved to St John's Street. When J.W. Moore died, the reins were taken by his son, H.W. Moore and his son-in-law P. Wingham, becoming known as Moore and Wingham by the 1920s. The 1930s and the Second World War brought many challenges and in 1945 the company joined with the growing local printing firm of Arthur Tillyer, the company henceforth being called Moore and Tillyer. The St John's Street printing works was known as The Regnum Press and remained in operation until 2003 but it was the East Street shop, which closed in 1996, that was the part of the business that, owing to its prominent location, was best known. It provided for all stationery needs, business and private, and the staff gave the sort of service that is rare on the High Street today, not infrequently finding what was needed tucked away in a drawer.

CHAFFER & SON, 1 Tower Street

For sixty years Chichester was also served by another centrally located printer: this was Chaffer, Son & Squibb, established in 1935 and situated at 1, Tower Street. Leonard Chaffer was the main investor in the firm and within a year, consequent on the death of Mr E.H. Squibb, it became known simply as Chaffer & Son. The Son was Leonard's son, Norman, who started as a junior but was still involved in the business when it closed in 1996. Looking at the account books (purchased at Moore and Wingham) from the early days it is evident that business was steady with people wanting letterheads and wedding stationery printed. There was also demand from many local firms including local Public Houses such as the Fleece Inn, the Bull Inn, the George and Dragon, and the Nag's Head for various printing jobs. The customer base expanded and the type of work requested also varied more, often reflecting the times. For example, in 1939 typical work was to produce one hundred Tontine Club cards for Eastgate Brewery but come September, and the outbreak of War, Chaffers were printing five thousand Rationing Leaflets and two thousand seven hundred and fifty Military Training Leaflets.

Leonard Chaffer had been a Printer's Assistant in the 1920s but by the time of his death in January 1953 he was running his own business and was a Master Printer. Norman Chaffer now ran the business and by July 1953 the registration of Norman and the Executors of Leonard Chaffer's will (namely Norman, his brother Alan and sister Cicely) as partners in Chaffer & Son was complete. Leonard Chaffer had arranged that the income from his share of the business went to his widowed wife during her life and after her death he bequeathed it to his son Norman, absolutely.

This was a business that had to innovate but one that also made a virtue of its heritage, especially its print shop that changed little from the 1930s. Indeed I remember

Fig. 10. The attractive private house appearance of Chaffer & Son

as a boy in the 1970s marvelling at the machine that could be seen through the window on Tower Street. In promotional artwork from 1979 this character was made clear with the firm proclaiming 'THE OLD AND THE NEW, Established in 1935.... in the old craft of Letterpress Printing but now SIDE BY SIDE with the modern Offset-Litho Printing.'

The family nature of the company is shown by the fact that Norman Chaffer's son, David, worked at the business for around twenty years and was running it with his father when it ceased its sixty years of trading towards the end of 1996. Sadly, the end came after a large investment in some machinery, which the firm subsequently believed to be defective. Chaffers pursued an unsuccessful court case and the costs incurred left them no alternative other than to close.

Each of the businesses outlined above are no longer part of the Chichester street scene. The people involved made their livelihoods by following their own individual paths but they all have something in common: they share the fact that they were successful at what they did, and in the process contributed to the function and richness of life for a Cicestrian. For that we should be thankful.

For assistance with particular aspects of the account, I am very grateful to John and Gabrielle Dent; to Viv Meynell; and to staff at WSRO who permitted scrutiny of a collection of presently uncatalogued items donated by the Chaffer family.

10
FEASTING THE EYE

MELISSA COX & PAUL FOSTER

Art is the unceasing effort to compete with the beauty of flowers
Gian Carlo Menotti (1911-2007)

The idea of 'feasting' has many associations, especially with food and grand occasions – state dinners and the like. By extension we often use the word to express pleasure that, in more ordinary circumstances, was unexpected – a picnic, perhaps, that was thought to be fairly ordinary but when revealed was found to include wild salmon, a collation of cold meats (duck as well as chicken), delicately spiced preserves, sweet biscuits and fruits, with marzipan and homemade cake to follow; or a barbecue say, where, expecting cold sausages and burnt burgers, one arrives to find half a pig roasting on an improvised spit in the garden, with the simple bonfire tended by an Argentine guacho – dressed for the role. This kind of extension of 'feast' is well understood, but in what follows there is concentration on a quite particular form of feasting – that intense, even embracing, pleasure that can be derived from flowers and from art.

When we think of decorating a room, it is usual to consider first its purpose, and from that to begin to select a colour scheme, furniture, and other furnishings such as carpets, cushions and so forth. But however satisfying the outcome, there is often a final stage to negotiate: what pictures to hang, what flowers to arrange or whether there is place, perhaps, for a sculpture. And it is the opportunities provided by Chichester in past years to satisfy this need that is the focus, but in a quite special way. Today we are becoming increasingly familiar with the phrase, 'virtual reality' (VR). Applied primarily to electronically-generated images on our computers and tablets, we have little difficulty differentiating what we see on our screens (however 'realistic' the image may seem), from actual reality; for we all know the difference between a computer image and the real thing. A similar distinction is necessary when we think of paintings, a sculpture, or flowers. A print of a famous work, of say, water-lilies by Monet, is best understood as equivalent to a VR image; in contrast, a painting that is original possesses a reality that can quicken the pulse and loosen the wallet to a quite extraordinary degree, Monet's *Le Bassin aux Nympheas* (one of his 'water landscapes', with lilies) selling in 2008 for over £40m. A similar distinction, although not at that kind of monetary level, may be made with flowers: a vase of freshly-picked delphiniums, interleaved with mignonette and myrtle – to give perfume, bearing no relation at all to artificial (dusty) sprays assigned to an hotel window or cafe table.

In acknowledgement of this distinction, the pages that follow will concentrate solely on three outlets at the top of their business – the David Paul Gallery, the Eastgate Gallery, and the South Street florist - Hooper's.

DAVID PAUL GALLERY - formerly 56, East Street, then Adelaide Road

The success or failure of a business is very dependent on the personalities of the principals involved; and this is especially so for an art gallery which, at its best, is more than just a business. In this instance, the relationship of the three principals involved was complex; yet, it was this relationship that created a gallery much loved by the exhibiting artists and by the visiting public.

Fig. 1. The David Paul Gallery, reaching along St John's Street and with another entrance and display window in East Street.

The gallery was established in 1960 by Connie Fox, David Goodman, and Connie's daughter, Shirley Fox, by initially renting the small building in St John's Street which had been a tailor's shop, 'The Tailor of Two Cities'; but the gallery soon took over the whole corner site, as the occupants , W.V. Knight –tobacconist downstairs, accounts upstairs – retired. The owner of the building used to live there as a child and often visited to recall childhood memories, but the gallery finally bought the whole site. The premises had a charming Victorian interior, and as many features as possible were kept and restored, including the wooden floors, the stone floor in the cellar, and a pretty Victorian stairway which wound up from the cellar to the top floor.

The gallery brought to Chichester an extraordinary number of nationally and internationally-recognized artists, who transcended the boundaries of the Chichester area. The initial opening in the early 1960s was startlingly successful. Invitations had been sent not knowing what to expect, but in the event so many people arrived that there was standing only, even on the pavement outside! This initial success set a trend for a provincial gallery and led considerable acclaim.

Fig. 2. John Aldridge R.A., Landscape in Abruzzo *(1965, Exhibition 1972)*

One great advantage that supported its success was its list of exhibitors, several of whom were locally based – R. O Dunlop R.A. for instance, John Hitchens, Eric James Mellon, and John Skelton. Of course, David Goodman was himself an artist, and there were several exhibitions of his work:* but many other artists were drawn from further afield.

The gallery, in fact, specialized in Modern British, but there were no fixed rules and a variety of work other than just paintings were shown – sculpture, ceramics, and original prints. Outstanding exhibitions included work by Edward Bawden, John Bratby, Eric Gill, Anthony Gross, Elisabeth Frink. Occasionally, group exhibitions were held: work by Royal Academicians, for instance (which included fourteen exhibitors), and work by children's book illustrators, notably Pauline Baynes, Quentin Blake, John Lawrence, and twenty-one other leading illustrators. Another indication of the taste exhibited by the gallery

Fig. 3. David Goodman, Still Life *(1972, Exhibition 1983)*

* For a full conspectus of David's contribution to the cultural life of Chichester, see *David Goodman: Artist and Essayist,* Chichester Modern Artists Two (University of Chichester, 2006).

Fig. 4. Elisabeth Frink, Bronze Boar *(Exhibition 1975)*

was the acclaim of critics and others, especially from London where the gallery established a strong link, for instance, with the Piccadilly Gallery. Indeed, outside the London area the David Paul Gallery was unique, and it would be difficult to repeat such a venture today. To run a gallery showing original work of the kind indicated for thirty years was no mean feat and many in the region, as well as farther afield, intensely regretted its eventual closure and relocation. This occurred when Connie Fox retired at the end of the 1980s, and David and Shirley sold the gallery and bought what was 'The Freezer Centre' in Adelaide Road,. Here they moved their other business, The David Paul Workshop (from The Hornet), and made bespoke period frames and some restoration work - mostly for London galleries. But in 2006 they closed the business, and sold the property: it has now been rebuilt as a number of townhouses.

EASTGATE GALLERY, 11 The Hornet

In 1967 Ken Child and Nigel Purchase founded what was later to become the Eastgate Gallery – it was first called 'The Art Cupboard' and consisted of a small boutique (approximately 8' x 4') in an antique market, located in an old eighteenth-century theatre in South Street . After a few years they moved location to a site opposite the old Shippham's Factory in the Sharp Garland buildings, East Walls, Chichester. Sharp Garland, an established grocers, were vacating the site as the buildings had become unsafe, just a few single storied out-buildings remained and Ken and Nigel were granted occupancy on the condition that they repaired these buildings. With Ken's knowledge of building structures it seemed a reasonable request; Ken had experience of restoring his own cottages and was at that time engaged as a stonemason restoring the City Market Cross. The window display for the Gallery was a square opening in the City Wall (you can see where the square opening was to this day, although it is now bricked in). Art was always going to be a meagre source of income, so they combined selling their art with taking in picture framing.

Then the inevitable happened – all the property was sold to a London property development company who began to redevelop, along with much of its other property in the City. The upshot was that Ken and Nigel were able to negotiate tenancy of a property in The Hornet – at the old Alms Houses. They named the space The Eastgate Gallery' and occupied these premises for five years, along with a good friend Bob Froud who restored and sold pine furniture in one of the other units. This establishment was what we would now described as 'shabby chic', but a more literal recollection is of walking through an overgrown backyard to a tumble down room where the prominent feature was the cast iron framed cutting guillotine. In a mountain beneath the guillotine lay hundreds of picture frame off-cuts smelling of freshly cut pine. Around the whitewash walls were paintings by Nigel and Ken. The highlight of the Gallery's selling cycle both then and in future years was always the 'private viewing' of the latest collection of art – these were by private invitation and attracted the patrons and local characters. The

Fig. 5. Ken Child, who helped prepare this account of the Gallery

Fig. 6. The Eastgate Gallery with Ken Child pictured in the doorway

wine flowed and the principals exuded an the eager anticipation of where the next 'red sales dot' would land as clients made their choices.

Ken and Nigel made their final move (just a few doors down) to the much more spacious accommodation of 11 The Hornet. This building had formerly been an agricultural machinery store for Goodrowes and has two very large doors which formerly had allowed access for machinery. These doors were fitted with a bell that jingled in a friendly tone as customers came in.

The Eastgate Gallery had two stories and plenty of wall hanging space which now included the work of other local artists – Peter Iden, Oliver Ommany, David Wade and the young artist Richard Webb, to name just a few. Then a most fortunate occurrence took place: some dear friends – Vivian and Patsy Meynell who had an antiquarian book shop in East Street had just been presented with a new lease, but it was so high they couldn't afford it. Nigel and Ken approached them and in no time at all upstairs at the Gallery became home to Meynells Bookshop.

The combination of art gallery below and antiquarian bookshop above was a happy one and customers enjoyed both the goods on sale and the lively personalities of Ken, Nigel, Viv and Patsy. The years together were punctuated with a great deal of laughter and fun, for the Meynells shared the same sense of humour as Nigel and Ken. This meant there was a lot of humourous shouting up and down the stairs! Ken, both an excellent artist and skilled stone mason who was responsible for the 1960s+ restoration of the Chichester Market Cross and letter cutting (an example of which can be seen in the Fitzalan Chapel at Arundel Castle, commemorating the life of Francis Steer), retired from The Eastgate Gallery in 1988.

Fig. 7. Christmas at The Eastgate Gallery, showing the fine staircase: in the centre of the picture Irene Purchase (Nigel's mother), to the right Melissa (daughter) and to the left Mary Cook (cousin of Nigel's father)

Nigel and his wife Martine, also an artist, continued to run the gallery. By now, Nigel had developed a reputation for his highly detailed Chichester Street scenes. Inspired by a painting of East Street in 1813 by a well-known artist of his time, Joseph Gilbert, Nigel took on the huge task of an opened perspective view of East Street peopled by 100 of the best known people of the city and district. In so doing he extended the original concept, and his own painting, completed in 1978, but set in 1977 as a tribute to HM The Queen's Jubilee Year, the painting was also a tribute to his native city. During his life he went on to paint South, North [for a detail, see page 73] and West Street in the same style. He also did commemorative paintings in this style of St Pancras Corporation, The Festival Theatre, The Prebendal School, The Bible Society (Swindon), Stansted House, Priory Park, Goodwood Race Course, Westbourne School House, and The Dolphin and Anchor Chichester. Across all such works, he featured almost 1500 Cicestrians, many of whom have entered the historical record solely because of Nigel's remarkable skill in miniature portraiture.

Nigel and Martine's son, Hugo, joined the family business in 1993 and learnt the picture framing trade. Hugo, also a talented artist, exhibited his work at the Gallery. Nigel eventually retired in 2006 and The Eastgate Gallery closed; however around the homes of West Sussex and beyond you will find many works of art that came from the local artists who once met and exhibited there.

Fig. 8. Nigel Purchase, East Street *(1978)*

Fig. 9. Nigel Purchase with his painting of the Dolphin & Anchor

Fig. 10. Nigel Purchase, 2 February 1940 – 21 May 2011

HOOPERS OF CHICHESTER – FLOWERS, 14 South Street

The retail flower trade, particularly throughout the first half of last century (and before that, of course) was dominated by local market gardeners. Chidham, for instance, possessed two notable businesses, one run the Hackett family, the other by Wakefords – and it was Henry Wakeford who ran a floristry business at 12 South Street (now part of Timothy Roe, Fine Jewellery) from at least 1930 into the 1950s. And there was also a florists at 5 South Street (part of what is now Quba & Co) which was run by Cecil Shippam from a nursery at Basin Road.[1]

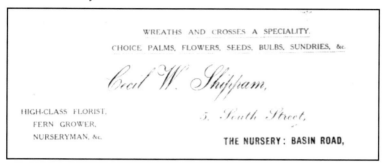

Fig. 11. Letterhead for Cecil W. Shippam's Nursery

But Wakeford's principal and long-standing competitor was situated further down South Street (from 1913 at 65 South Street – now the Barnardo's outlet, but from 1930 to at least the early 1970s at 32a Southgate[2]): this was Websters, who possessed the enormous advantage of being able to supply the shop from their nursery in Market Avenue.

Websters nursery was not the sole nursery in Chichester; indeed, the city was almost surrounded by nurseries at all points of the compass. The most dramatic was Northgate Nurseries, a nursery run by Miss H. J. McRonald. Established almost a century earlier, it extended over six acres and had the finest collection of roses in the county. Miss McRonald (b.1859) was elected FRHS in 1894.[3] Occupying the entire ground of what we now know at

Fig. 12. Websters' shop front at 32a Southgate

1 Cecil was one of the eleven children of Charles Shippam, the founder of the East Street factory. Cecil was also photographer to the firm, and lived at 11 North Pallant with his sister, Freida.

2 Now renumbered as 33, and occupied by Gemini

3 James McRonald (1819-1895) at the time of his death had run the nursery for about thirty years; the nursery passed to his daughter, Helen, but his presence is still active amongst us as in March 2007 his copy of E.J. Lowe, *Ferns - British and Exotic* (1856 - bought that same year by McRonald and immediately dated and autographed), was sold at auction in Sydney, Australia.

Fig. 13. McRonald's fine classical pavilion at the heart of his nursery; the building, much changed, still survives (from Views and Reviews *(special edition) Chichester – c. 1896 W.T. Pike & Co., Brighton)*

the Northgate Circulatory. But our attention must move south-east for there, on the Bognor Road, just beyond the Wickham Arms, was the Peacheries which Maurice Evans (d. January 2009) inherited from his father and where the produce included fruit as well as flowers. In fact Maurice Evans' grandfather, George Sidney Evans (d. 1939) had run the business since 1913 and grown it to become the largest peachery in the country, with 48 glasshouses containing over 600 trees (see *Chichester Observer* 18 Nov. 1939). Most of the produce went to markets at Brighton or Covent Garden in London, but from 1953 there was also a small shop at 21, The Buttermarket in North Street. Later in the 1950s, the years of the expanding British economy and when Harold Macmillan pronounced at Bedford in July 1957 that the country 'had never had it so good', Maurice received a compelling offer from a developer for the nursery – and, looking elsewhere, decided in 1960 to take a 50-50 business partner, Mrs Jean Siviter. They divided responsibilities with Maurice looking after the buying and bookkeeping while Jean handled the display and the training of assistants in the art of floristry, giving particular attention to skills of self-presentation and to customer service. The partnership worked extremely well as they were each very good in their own sphere, Jean's son writing recently (e-communication to present writer, 8 July 2011), attributing this to 'Mother being a very good ex-infant school teacher while Maurice was very good in communication with other growers in buying [and] also adamant that the day's takings had to balance to the nearest penny'.

Soon the business outgrew the small shop in the North Street Buttermarket and in 1962, determining to expand but retain the Buttermarket shop, they approached the Dean and Chapter to rent 14 South Street (now the fashion retailer, East Ltd, but at the time a branch of Charge & Co.). It was here that things really progressed for there was extensive floor space to sell from, workroom bench space to produce hand made items and also a very cool cellar for storage of all the incoming cut flowers. (The cellar used to, and still does, run right out to the middle of South Street with very old stonework and fine brickwork – seen by the present writer, courtesy East Ltd.) Fresh flowers only had cellar life of one day, and if they didn't make the shop in that time they were used in other ways. This is where the shop's name for good flowers came from, in conjunction of course with careful buying, strict rotation and teaching of the skills to the assistants.

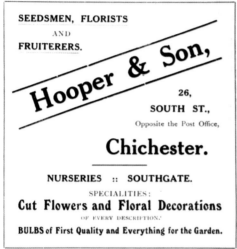

Fig. 14. Hooper & Son full-page advertisement in The Official Guide to Chichester *(W.H. Barrett, c. 1911)*

Hoopers of Chichester, for this was the name they traded under,[4] was always a member of Interflora, and as the business prospered, both Maurice and Jean became interested in the local area group and eventually joined the national group. As Jonathan Siviter wrote (cited above), 'Mother was the editor of the national quarterly journal for several years but then became interested in the teaching side.[5] She was responsible for setting up the residential course at Brinsbury Agricultural College north of Pulborough, and later the full time course at Chichester College. She took a great deal of interest in the students,

---

4 This trading name has a long and intriguing history: a John Hooper, a native of Salisbury, came to Chichester with his wife, Martha, a Pembrokeshire girl, c. 1878-80 as shopman to James McDonald, seedsman of 65 South Street. Initially he lived over the shop but by the end of the century he was trading on his own account at 26 South Street. Although Hooper died in 1926, the business (which had been trading as Hooper & Son) was continued by his son, Earnest, and two daughters, Eleanor and Florence, at 27 South Street until after WW2. In 1947 the three principals retired and the firm was bought by the Evans family, the name 'Hooper' being transferred to the nursery business at the Peacheries and, when that was sold, used for the retail business.

5 And still, at over ninety years, when I visited her earlier this year, emphasizing the importance she attached to staff in the shop taking the necessary examinations to gain proper qualification and professional status; she was also reading the latest Interflora journal. *PF.*

always trying to employ one every year'. Expansion of the business led to a considerable staff role, the firm employing for a long time twenty-six full time and five part time staff, and were acknowledged locally as 'good employers'.

For several years Jean taught at the National Conference held in Blackpool, at Blackpool Tower; able to talk and demonstrate at the same time, she gained great respect from Jimmy Young who worked alongside her to entertain the huge audience, as well as forwarding the occasion by asking pertinent questions himself.

Jonathan records that he was always expected to help out at busy times, Valentine' Day, Mothering Sunday, Easter and at the Christmas period by delivering flowers and bouquets. When engaged in this way, often with four other drivers similarly engaged, his area was west as far as Emsworth and north as far as South Harting, but no further east than Goodwood. In reminiscing, he writes that 'Mother and I still joke that for Valentine's Day I could deliver 50 red roses to 50 different houses and cover 50 miles. It sounds strange economics but it was the name of the game for Interflora'.

The firm finally closed in the early 1980s, and new businesses started up – for instance, S & L Flowers (first in East Street, now in Eastgate Square), Blooms – at 3A Little London and founded in 1991, and The Flower Gallery at 54 North Street (founded c. 1995); and earlier this year Wild Rose in West Street. Each of these firms, and let us hope the latest will join them, has traded successfully over several decades, and although the initial stages may have been taxing, they would probably all agree with the poet, William Cowper (1731-1800) that, although

The bud may have a bitter taste,

. . . sweet [will be] the flow'r.

Particular thanks in this chapter are due to Shirley Fox for her revisions to earlier texts about the history of the David Paul Gallery; to Rosey Purchase, and Hugo Purchase; and to Jean Siviter and John Hooper.

Fig. 15. Lilium longifolum *enjoying summer 2011 on a Sussex steddle*

11
SILVER AND GOLD

JULIE & KEITH MASTERS

Make new friends, but keep the old;
those are silver, these are gold.

Joseph Parry

When one thinks of gold and silver, immediately jewellery springs to mind, and from that the countless jewellers' shops in the city. Some are in retail chains with branches nationwide, whilst others are very individual. There is a very large number in Chichester, and they all have gold and silver in some form or other in their windows. The retail chains tend to follow a pattern with identical displays, but some of the privately owned ones are eye-catching and artistic, depending on the skill and flair of the owner. For instance, at Timothy Roe's shop in South Street the windows are

Fig.1. Allen's shop front with its 'coronation streamers' and GR on the wall above (12 May1937). The proprietor at the time, Charles Cousins Allen, stands fourth from the left (with three male employees further left); to the right of Allen is first Robert Allen, then Ronald Allen, a daughter (Mariota) and five female assistants

lined with black and purple, which shows off the gold and silver in a very attractive manner. Others are more traditional, with rows of watches in one section, while ring pads are displayed in another and bangles, necklaces and chains with pendants take up another part of the window. In the 1937 Coronation photo of C.C. Allen, it shows how cluttered their windows were, being keen to show as many goods as possible.

Of all the trades that once could be found within the city walls, for example butchers, bakers and fishmongers, it often seems as if only the jewellers have survived. In the '50s, the shops were situated thus: North Street: Whiteheads near the Crooked S; Rogers (now Nationwide Building Society); East Street: Faith's (now Body Shop); Lewis's (now Fat Face); South Street: Robert Allen (now Cath Kidston); C.C. Allen (now Past Times and Rowlands of Bath).

In this article, however, we are concentrating on two jewellers' shops from the past because one is where Keith was trained and worked for 21 years from 1950 to 1971 in all three parts of the trade: clockmaking, watchmaking and jewellery. Keith has many memories of things he observed and tales he was told by older employees, some long since passed away.

CHARLES C. ALLEN, 57-59 South Street

Charles C. Allen was born in 1872 and died in 1958 aged 86. His father, also Charles, was a 'bootmaker master' working from West Street, but CC started as an apprentice at Faith's jewellers in East Street and then went to London to complete his training. He opened a shop at 31 Southgate in 1905 (now Lucky House – a Chinese Takeaway) and moved along to 59 South Street in 1909. In the 1920s he bought 57 and 58, so he then owned all three adjoining shops. He also owned 8 South Street, and during the war, when goods were scarce, he sold leather goods there as well as jewellery. His son Charles Ronald and his daughter Mariota Prudence (but known as Maisie), took over the business when he died, having been trained by him in the shop, although Ron did very little in the workshop by way of repairs.

During his lifetime Charlie Allen was mayor twice (1933-34, then 1934-35); and both father and son took part in civic duties. During his working life Ronnie was always to be seen in the shop and became known as 'Shake-hands-Allen' because he shook the hand of every customer on arrival and on departure.

The family lived in the flat upstairs, over 57-59, until they moved to a large house at Westgate, and Charlie could often be heard calling to his family using nicknames. His wife, Kate, was called Tit, Ronnie was Boy, and Maisie was Girlie. Ron and Maisie died in 1993, within three months of each other.

The shop at 57-59 South Street was a large unit with two doors, but only one was used, to enter the main shop area. The unused door led into the antiques section, and to enter this one had to pass through the main shop. This area was used to store a jumble of second-hand goods untidily displayed. It had a certain air of mystery, for if a member of staff needed to be spoken to privately they were taken into the antiques section and the door was closed, making for a secretive atmosphere!

As one entered the main door there was a glass counter on the left, from behind which shop assistants served customers. Over this counter, on the left was the naked flame used for sealing the parcels with sealing wax. This area was lit by two light bulbs, each being only 120 watts. If one blew, the other needed replacing also: these were specially obtained and very gloomy.

Fig. 2. Maisie Allen in c. 1986 and, right, her brother Ron.

It was at this counter that most of the jewellery and the antiques were priced with a code which was ABC PRINGLE. Pringle's was the name of a wholesale firm in London: therefore A=1, B=2, C=3, P=4, R=5, I=6, N=7, G=8, L=9, E=0. The shop girls did all the coding. All invoices were pierced onto a metal hook, which made for a very antiquated filing system!

The premises had very little heating, just black paraffin stoves. The front door of the shop was left open throughout the year, whatever the weather, to encourage customers in: this meant the shop assistants were frozen. Ron and Maisie kept their coats on and if customers commented on this they said they were too busy to stop and remove them.

There was a passage through to the two workshops where repairs were carried out. In 1950, when Keith arrived as an apprentice, the heating was a one-bar electric fire. Charlie Allen was by now in his eighties and kept a strict no-talking policy, maintaining that if you were talking you were not working! The first workshop was where the two watchmakers sat. In the next one, through a door, was a clockmaker, an improver and Keith, the apprentice. At the far end of this long room was the jeweller. Apprentices were trained in all three skills, starting with alarm clocks. There was a sink in the room, and electrical polishing equipment which caused considerable dust. In the late 50s another room was built on, and the sink and polishing equipment were transferred there.

There was no hot water, only a cold tap. If hot water was required, it was boiled in a saucepan on a free-standing gas ring. Toilet facilities were minimal. For the workmen there was a toilet with no window or light, just a door, in the far corner of the garage. The shop girls were allowed to use the facilities in the living accommodation.

There were cellars in the shop, where the coal for the living quarters was kept. It was the job of the apprentice to bring up the coal. He also had to mop the shop floor and wash the pavement and windows every Monday morning. One poor apprentice was caught out. Before the war, Charlie went regularly to London and on one occasion, before he left, he wiped his fingers along the windows. On his return he asked the apprentice if he had cleaned the windows; the answer was, "Yes, sir!" but Charlie proceeded to show the poor fellow the finger marks he had made the previous morning! On another occasion the jeweller accidentally snapped a silver hairbrush. He called the family dog into the workshop, put the brush in the dog's mouth and sent it outside into the garden. On hearing the commotion, Charlie chased the poor creature round, blaming it for the broken brush!

In the 50s, when Keith began work, there was a strict ritual for receiving one's wages. At 6 p.m. on Saturdays all the staff lined up in order, starting with the juniors at the front and finishing with the most senior member last of all. The money was paid over the counter by Maisie, who counted the cash into one's hand. She would not pay the next in line until the previous person had left. This being so, no one knew what the person behind received, so we never discovered what the senior man was paid!

Up until the 1950s, jewellers' shops also traded as opticians. A rod and sliding lens was used to test the strength of the lens required and then the spectacles were made up. Broken spectacles were often brought in for repair and, once repaired, the workman tried them on in front of a mirror to make sure they sat correctly on one's nose. After one pair was repaired, Mr Hunt, the carrier, collected them and returned them to a customer who lived in the country. The next day, Mr Hunt returned the spectacles to Charlie, who took them into the workshop and asked the workman if he had tried them on. He said he had, but was asked to do so again only to find that the arms were upside down and the loops went upwards!

One of the clockmakers, Harold Smith, started his apprenticeship in the 1920s and, apart from war service, remained working for the Allens until the shop closed in the '80s. He was the only member of staff to achieve this, being employed by them the whole of his working life.

C.C. Allen's was a reputable and reliable establishment, which existed for most of the twentieth century and was typical of the Edwardian period, remaining unchanged till the day it closed; but its influence (essentially that of the Allens) is still current in the City. At the present time, Timothy Roe (whose premises are at 12-13 South Street) worked at Allen's; and, when the Allens closed their shop, Simon Tilley (now of Ebony Jewellers, 20 South Street), was one who helped to clear the premises and transfer items to the Allens' home at Westgate. But there existed another jewellery shop in South Street, trading also under the name Allen; this was Robert Allen's shop at 24A (later 24) South Street, almost opposite C.C. Allen's. In fact, Robert (1882-1944) was a blood relative to Ronald and Mariota Allen and, after his early death, staff at Allens in the 1950s, when Robert Allen's was being run by a W. & S.A. Darby (although still trading under the name Robert Allen), were instructed to have nothing to do with the shop! Such rivalry, if that was what it was, is however mere speculation.

Fig. 3. Queen Mary leaving 24A South Street in 1927

A.J. FAITH, 34-35 East Street

The history of this firm stretches back at least to 1833, and even earlier for a G. Faith is listed in 1823 as a watchmaker, silversmith and jeweller at High Street in Somerstown. The firm was not to close until 'Mr Derek' Faith retired in 1980, by which time it had traded from the same premises for 147 years – which is the Chichester record for a firm occupying the same premises and trading continuously.

Post WW2 the shop was run by Derek Faith and his wife, Irene, with one full-time assistant, Tony Puzey, and occasional help from a Miss Hoare. In the background, 'ruling with a rod of iron', was 'old Mrs Faith'. Tony's widow, recalls that her husband gained his position on leaving the RAF after the war. Prior to his war service he had worked at a watch and clock shop in the centre of Windsor and been responsible for the regular winding of clocks at the Castle. His main duties at Faith's were repairs – to watches and clocks.

Fig. 4. Shop front of A.J. Faith in c. 1975

Sadly, his loyalty to the firm was not to be rewarded by a long retirement, as he died in 1981, having been ill for several years before.

But if the Allen's endured for almost a century, and Faith's for much longer, mention must also be made of the present firm R L Austen at 75 North Street. Situated in the

Fig. 5. Interior to AJ Faith, with 'Mr Derek' (left), Mrs Irene Faith, and Tony Puzey

heart of historic Chichester, R.L. Austen Ltd. is an independent, family-run jewellers dating back to 1794, trading originally in East Street under the name E.H. Lewis. The business was bought by 'Dickie' Austen, a Fighter Pilot and gemologist in September 1964, and the name was changed to R.L. Austen Ltd. The firm was one of the first independent jewellers in the U.K. to stock Rolex watches, and has continued to do so now for over 40 years.

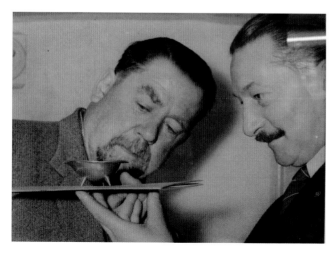

Fig. 6. Richard Austen (right) displaying a piece of silver for the artist, R.O Dunlop, RA. (c. 1975)

12
HARNESSING POWER
(Pedal, battery, electric & bee!)

PAUL FOSTER & SHEILA HALE

[Two] things greater than all things are:
…Horses and Power…
(Rudyard Kipling, *Ballad of the King's Jest*)

Although developed much earlier, it was not until the early 1930s, with the combination of rising wages and falling production costs, that the bicycle (already a popular form of transport) became more affordable for working people. The diamond frame, equal sized wheels, and straight handlebar design had remained basically the same since 1890 for the man in the street, but during the first half of the 20th century innovations took place in the running gear, and introduction of quick release wheels, derailleur gears and cable-operated brakes were welcomed by the enthusiastic Club Riders; even more appreciated by them was the introduction of aluminium alloy for wheel rims, handlebars and seat posts which greatly reduced the weight of bicycles for competitive sport..

After the decline of horse-drawn vehicles and hand-carts, the tradesmen's carrier cycles became very popular for door to door deliveries, especially after petrol rationing came into force. Different models were produced to suit various trades and the name of the business was emblazoned on the wide crossbar. On Saturdays schoolchildren were employed to do the deliveries and it was not unusual to see the boy / girl butcher's basket piled high with joints of meat or strings of sausages (barely wrapped and the bill secured with a metal skewer) closely followed by a posse of dogs hoping for a juicy morsel to fall off. At the beginning of the round the load was so heavy that it was difficult to find a secure place to stand the bike whilst making a delivery and, if any meat was lost or the money to be collected didn't tally, the boy / girl had to make good! Once the basket was empty it was back to the shop for a refill and another round was started.

The word, wireless, derived from the 'wireless telegraph', was the most common term used for a radio up until the 1960s. By the 1930s the wireless set was no longer an experimental apparatus, nor was it the enthusiast's toy, and shops opened selling and repairing wireless sets. Some were extensions of existing businesses – often cycle shops or even ironmongers. At first few people could afford to own a ready-made wireless set so many bought self-assembly kits. As electricity was not readily available in most houses, the sets required the use of batteries, usually lead acid cells, which needed recharging and the replacement of the electrolyte (mild sulphuric acid) which was supplied to the shop in glass bottles or carboys. The manufacture of domestic wireless sets virtually stopped at the outbreak of War in September 1939, as the factories had to turn their attention to the production of wireless and radar equipment for the Armed Forces. Prior to the 1960s all radios used valves, a glass tube with electrodes visible inside, which needed very high voltage to operate and, in turn, required a substantial multi-cell battery but by the middle of that decade 'solid state' (i.e. transistorised equipment) became increasingly common.

A ANDREWS, cycle agent and dealer; and sports depot, 14 (or 13) North Street

There is no entry for this business in 1905 but in the 1909 Directory, Alfred Andrews,

is to be found at 14 North Street, listing himself as a cycle agent and dealer, and sports depot and it remained in the same family for over eighty years. It is interesting to read the entries through the years as they indicate the changes taking place up to 1971 the latest seen by me. Unfortunately Trade Directories were no longer printed after the mid-1970s.

A full page advertisement in 1930 contains an illustration of their trade mark and is offering

Fig. 1. Andrews shop in North Street - from Kelly's 1930 Directory of Chichester

The Rival "A" Cycles from £3.19.6d (15 models to select from) and states that they are 'Agents for Rudge-Whitworth, Ariel, Fleet, Swift, New Hudson, Three Spires and B.S.A. Hire Purchase arranged. All models. Each machine supplied complete with inflator, tool bag and spanners. For an extra 5/- a policy will be issued covering Rider and Machine against accident.

In that year Mr. Andrews is also selling wireless and musical instruments. His advertisement in the 1933 edition is all about 'Wireless! Wireless!! Wireless!!! As the sole distributor of Silver Knight High Tension Batteries etc.' By 1954 the shop is listed as selling 'Power Pak' bicycle motors, Humber,

Fig. 2. Advertising page from a Chichester Directory

Robin Hood and Elswick cycles. Another ten years later it is cycles and electrical appliances and, within another four years motor accessories have been added.

In the Nigel Purchase North Street painting commemorating the 25th anniversary of the twinning of Chartres with Chichester in 1984, there is an image of Roy Andrews 'retired cycle shop owner'.

CHITTY BROS. LTD., electrical and cycle shop, 28 North Street

The Chitty family were well-known in Chichester and the surroundings villages where they had lived for generations as farmers and shopkeepers. Whilst some members of the family still live in the area, they are no longer occupied as previously.

Arthur Harold Chitty was born at Saltham Farm, Runcton, in 1906 and was educated at the Prebendal School. On leaving school he worked in his grandfather Jarman's, grocery business in North Street – on the site once occupied by Woolworths, currently Boots.

In the 1930s Harry Hewitt is listed in Directories as a cycle agent at 26 North Street, on the corner of North Street and Crane Street (now called Sussex House and housing a hairdressing business). A couple of years later the occupants are shown as Boyce and Chitty, wireless

Fig. 3. Chitty Brothers at 28 North Street

dealers although they still had the cycle agencies. By 1950, Arthur Harold's older brother was working in the shop, and the name had changed to Chitty Bros. Ltd. The 1964 Directory shows that at some time between these two dates they had moved the business along the road to 28 North Street (now an Oak Furniture outlet). These premises were double fronted with a recessed door. Displayed on the inside of the side windows were pots of honey and honeycombs, seemingly rather unusual commodities to find in a cycle and electrical shop! Inside among the latest bicycles, baskets, saddlebags, lamps and torches, spools of electrical wires of varying circumferences and colour, batteries, radios, televisions, and other household appliances, together with all the accoutrements of such a business, was to be found bee keeping equipment for sale and a display of certificates of excellence awarded to Arthur Harold Chitty for his expertise in bee keeping.

His life long interest in bees began rather dramatically when he was about 16 and inadvertently drove his motor-cycle through a swarm of bees causing him to fall off his machine. He was fascinated by the way a beekeeper, who came to collect the swarm, was able to handle and calm them. He had his first apiary at 'Sunnyside', Hunston, where his father had a brick-kiln, and the last one at School Lane, North Mundham, which he maintained, with the help of friends, until his death in 1996. At one time he had over 100 hives spread around the county from which he had to collect honey, and maintain and feed the colonies, having established an arrangement with a number of private landowners and estates whereby he could place his hives on their land in return for honey as rent! He was recognised throughout West Sussex for his knowledge of bee keeping and during the war he became a Bee Inspector for the Ministry of Food. He travelled to Japan, China and New Zealand in order to attend International Bee-keeping Conferences during his later years. As well as selling new bicycles and electrical goods, Chitty Bros. Ltd. offered a repair service for these items and also undertook electrical contracts. They secured several tenders from the Ministry of Defence, one of which was for the installation of landing lights at Ford aerodrome for the RAF.

Arthur Harold Chitty was married to Dora Vick, the daughter of another well-known Chichester business family.

STENNING'S CYCLE SHOP, 43 Spitalfield Lane

Cliffie George Stenning ran the village grocer's shop in East Dean before moving with his family at the beginning of the 20th century to Spitalfield Lane, Chichester. The lane then was a far cry from the road as we know it today, as there were then only two other houses in the area. One of these, 'Whymark', was occupied by Alderman Apps; the second, Spitalfield House, a strangely shaped building, was occupied by a Mr John Pullen, his wife and family. He was known locally as 'Ducky' Pullen and travelled everywhere in his pony and trap. Mr. Pullen also owned a number of other fields and meadows and, later, some of these were sold to become Bridge Road, Armadale Road, and part of Green Lane. His land, fronting St. James' Road, became the site of St. James' Infants School in 1936. Spitalfield House was later pulled down and more houses were built on that land.

The Stenning family home, and the adjoining building which would become the cycle shop, was originally part of the Spitalfield Farm buildings and in the front garden of No 250 Spitalfield Lane (later renumbered as No. 41) was a very cold well, the water being extracted by a pump housed in an outhouse. The Prebendal School playing field was behind the property (now covered by St. Richard's Hospital) and the boys would make a beeline for a cold drink of water from the well at the completion of their sporting activities.[1]

---

[1] In his History of the Prebendal School (1984), Neville Ollerenshaw quotes Dorian Prince, a pupil from the 1920s, who became an Architect and served with the Royal Engineers in World War Two, who 50 years later, is remembering this 'playing' field '...we played cricket in a meadow near where St. Margaret's Hospital [St. Richards] now stands and before each game we had to shovel-up the cowpats and cut the pitch with a hand mower from grass and buttercups about 12 inches high. Hardly conducive to a high score but of great assistance to the bowlers'.

The cycle shop, established by Cliffie George Stenning in 1909 was taken on by his three sons, Roy, Cyril and David, when he died in 1959. After a while Roy, left the family firm to become an independent local representative for Kleeneze and by the time of his retirement he had become the firm's longest serving representative and much respected in the area.

Cyril and David Stenning continued to run the cycle dealer and repair business. There was always a religious text left in the saddlebag or basket when the repairs were completed - evidence of their strong faith.

Fig 4. David Stenning – outside the shop in Spitalfield Lane. The shop finally closed in 2005 and the premises are now used by an Undertaker.

* * *

There were numerous other cycle and electrical shops, all of which gave equally good service to their customers. For instance:

T. C. Daniels, 3 Northgate, electrical engineer (his van, with the electric loud hailer on top, was a familiar sight patrolling the streets during Election campaigns and other public events); C. G. Daughtry (proprietors H. F. Smart & W. A. V. Webber), radio, electrical and cycle engineers and dealers; Mrs. E. E Gardiner, 68 East Street, cycle agent, from early 1900s to late 1950s; Hoad & Holder, 156 St. Pancras, cycle agents, motor accessories and clothes, Triang toys (took over these premises from John Leng & Sons (Chichester) Ltd. c. 1950- c. mid 1970s); Norman Huggett, 110a The Hornet, electrical, radio and TV engineer and dealer; J. M. Selsby, 16 Westgate and 63 St. Paul's Road, electrical, radio and television engineer and contractor (private recording service); and R. C. Willmer, 23 North Street, radio, electrical and television engineer. But one of the most influential (if one thinks internationally) is H. E. Willard & Sons, 44 West Street, electrical engineers and contractors, later WILLARD ELECTRICAL at 48 South Street.

WILLARDS, 49 South Street

The history of this Chichester family firm almost mirrors the use of electricity and merits inclusion in the volume because of its historic retail presence; but the Willard family story is also fascinating in its own right for it is a beacon of achievement with an international profile, which continues to grow to this day.

Fig 5. Willards in South Street

Herbert (Bert) Willard was a keen radio enthusiast and built radio sets in the 1920s.[2] He was a trained engineer and began his own electrical business during the 1930s, during which he undertook the electrical wiring of many new houses on the well-known estates at Rose Green and Pagham, as well as many houses in the Chichester area. He was joined in 1948 by his son Jack Willard who had served an engineering apprenticeship in Portsmouth but had also served in the Royal Navy as an electrical artificer, a period during which he learned many of his electrical engineering skills. Father and son began trading from the family home in Salthill Road, Fishbourne, and mainly concentrated on industrial electrical engineering; but they soon found the need for commercial premises and rented space at 44 West Street, which at that time was also the location of Chichester Dairies.

By 1952 they had out grown the space at West Street and moved to a brand new building on the newly-formed Terminus Road Industrial Estate. The firm continued to grow and expand throughout the 1950s. During 1959 both Jack and his father successfully negotiated the purchase in Chichester of a leading electrical contracting and retailing company following the death of the proprietor, the firm was called T.F. Lummus, which Lummus had established at 49 South Street in the 1920s.

On the 1st January 1960, the Willard family took over the running of the electrical shop, although the name T.F. Lummus was to remain over the door until late into the 1970s. By the mid 1980s the emerging retail giants with their huge buying power were having their effect on many small electrical retailers and Willards could no longer compete on price. The decision was made to close the shop in February 1987 and the firm moved their sales operation to their trade counter on Terminus Road.

But the firm's standing rested not solely on its retail and trade activity, for in the mid 1950s a customer visited Jack in his workshop: she was a trainee paintings conservator at the Courtauld Institute in London, but lived in Chichester, and she needed a special

---

[2] His father, Godfrey Willard, was a sergeant in the Chichester police, and it may be that Herbert's interest in radio was stimulated by communication needs within the police.

Fig. 6. Jack Willard (right) and Paul – the current Managing Director

tool to help her with her work. Jack agreed to design and make the tool for her. This was a great success and soon other conservators wanted the same type of tools. It is from this invention that a new side of the Willard business grew throughout the 1960s & 1970s. Jack's son, Paul Willard, joined him in the business in 1981 and throughout the 80s & 90s they ran both the electrical and the conservation businesses together, Paul on streamlining and expanding the electrical contracting business, and Jack on developing new products: it was this specialist and growing world-class activity that led the firm to be consultants at Hampton Court and at Windsor Castle after the disastrous fires (1986 at the former, 1992 at the latter), and in 1992 to the award of a Royal Warrant from HM The Queen. By the year 2000, Jack was in his 70s and it was decided to sell off the electrical contracting business, allowing Paul to concentrate on the family's core skills of engineering and innovation. Jack Willard was awarded an MBE for his services to conservation and sadly passed away in 2007.

Paul Willard continues in his father's footsteps and currently runs the family manufacturing business with a small team of highly skilled technicians: they export their innovative Willard Conservation products to conservators within some of the world's most famous Art Galleries, Archives, Museums and private collections.

Grateful thanks in preparing this chapter to: John Grant, for information on bicycles; to Paul Willard; and to the resources at West Sussex Record Office: MP1966 (account of Chitty family); MP 4569 'Reminiscences of Portfield 1920s-1940s' by Geoff Farndell; MP 5262 (re. Roy Stenning); PH 18920 (Stenning Cycle Shop); (Chi. Obs. 15.09.2005 – Stenning).

13
PILLS AND POTIONS

Paul Foster

Man may escape from rope and gun;
But scarce will outlive the doctor's pill.
(Adapted from John Gay)

Keeping fit and healthy is a prime objective in human life. As an objective it is supported by three agencies: hospitals - for major and emergency intervention, doctors' surgeries - for initial diagnoses, and chemists' shops. This chapter is concerned solely with the last.

The term 'chemist's', in the sense of somewhere we go for medicine, is today often termed a *pharmacy* which, for those who know a little Greek makes its purpose very clear since its meaning stretches back at least to the Mycenaean Greek, *pamako* (pharmakon) – which can mean a drug or poison. The first recorded pharmacists are usually associated with Islamic culture as long ago as the eighth century (CE), and then in Islamic Spain from the twelfth century onwards; for us in England, though, we will be more familiar with the idea of the early apothecaries[1] (The Worshipful Society of Apothecaries of London were incorporated by Royal Charter under James I in 1617) and of Nicholas Culpeper's *Complete Herbal* (1653).

With the development of medical knowledge and an increasing focus on care (many of our most famous hospitals were founded in the eighteenth century – for instance, Guy's within Southwark in 1721; Addenbrooke's at Cambridge in 1766), greater scrutiny began to be applied to 'pills and potions' and in 1841 the [Royal] Pharmaceutical Society of Great Britain was founded to regulate the training of pharmacists, and to maintain standards[2] almost a generation before the establishment in 1858 of a similar body (what we now know as The General Medical Council) for the regulation of doctors.[3]

In order to train pharmacists, the Pharmaceutical Society established several Schools and the most immediate for our interest is the *Portsmouth and Gosport School of Science and the Arts*, which was established in 1869 and is now the University of Portsmouth – as it is there that many local pharmacists received their training, for instance George

---

[1] Derived from the French, *apotecaire*, meaning a place where wine, spices and herbs were stored: to go to a chemist's shop in Scandinavia today one is often directed to the 'apotek'
[2] Queen Victoria granted the Society a Royal Charter in 1843, but it was not until 1988 that our present Queen permitted the inclusion of 'Royal' in the Society's title. Earlier regulation had occurred in the Apothecaries Act of 1819
[3] This was when the term, General Practitioner (GP), came into existence, doctors prior to 1858 being regulated (in London at least) by the College of Physicians (1518), although the first semblance of regulation occurred in 1511 when bishops were required to regulate the work of physicians

Bevis of The Eastgate Pharmacy. Cicestrians will know that Sidney Bastow and The Eastgate Pharmacy were not the sole pharmacies in Chichester in, say, 1960, for in North Street there was also Binns (c. 1950-73 – now Grants Dry Cleaning), and in South Street there was Savory and Moore, as well as Boots the Chemist – with its library!

SIDNEY BASTOW LTD, 9, North Street and later 50-50a North Street

The Bastows, grandfather and father (both Sidney William) and then son (Timothy), offered Cicestrians services as dispensing chemists for almost a century. Their first

location at 9 North Street (recently Sussex Stationers, but now owned by W.H. Smith) was purchased by Sidney William Bastow in 1903, the property having previously been occupied for most of the intervening years by the family of John Phillipson who is recorded on the site in 1786 as an apothecary. Sidney died in 1930 but his son, also Sidney William, had married Phyllis Dallyn of the Hunston farmers of that name, and Timothy was born in 1935. Although his father had trained at the London School of Pharmacy (The Square, since it was situated in Bloomsbury Square) and was awarded the Pereira Silver medal, Timothy trained as a pharmacist at Brighton School of Pharmacy; now part of the University of Brighton and housed in

Fig. 1. The Frontage of 9 North Street in c. 1913

the Huxley Building – named after the renowned nineteenth century biologist, Thomas H. Huxley, whose aphorisms have resonated across a century and more since his death in 1895 - 'God give me strength to face a fact though it slay me', and 'Try to learn something about everything and everything about something'.

In 1985, Timothy Bastow, despite having been born at the property and holding it in considerable affection (he still comments

Fig. 2. An upstairs fireplace still extant in 2011

Fig. 3. 50-50a North Street: left – prior to Timothy acquiring the property and, right – with the new Bastow frontage

about the fine fireplaces), sold 9 North Street to the Church Commissioners and moved to 50 North Street. This property, at the time a Fish Restaurant had traded in fish since at least 1913 and required extensive refurbishment to make it habitable as a chemist's shop.

One of the advantages of the new premises was a more convenient location for the music department. This aspect of trading had been initiated by Timothy a number of years after the closure of Austin Storry's late in the 1960s. Storry's, at 83 North Street (now JD Sports), was situated almost directly opposite Bastow's at 9, North Street and was a large and successful music shop dealing not only in television and radio equipment, but also in every aspect of sheet music and records, as well as piano tuning and repairs; in addition, the shop housed a recording studio and became a popular centre for pupils to take the grade examinations of Trinity College of Music (founded in 1872). Timothy had no intention of replicating such a business, but he did see the opportunity to add records and other forms of

Fig. 4. Storry's frontage adjacent to the Market Hall.

music to his business – and dug out a cellar at 9 North Street for the purpose. As Manager, he appointed Ralph Harvey who had worked at the famous London store Discurio (situated then in Shepherd Street, Mayfair), and the new facility opened on 1 November 1981. So appreciated was Harvey's contribution to the business that it was

Fig. 5. An interior view of 9 North Street, with (left) Sidney Bastow, Timothy's father, and (right) Bernard Martin, a long-standing assistant. A Bastow daughter, Mary Florence (sister to Timothy's father and the future wife of Richard Doman), was a trained pharmacist and also worked in the shop.

component of the firm at the new premises – and acquired its own subsidiary address, becoming Bastow's Classics, 50a North Street, at which Ralph still assists.

More recently the family sold the assets and goodwill of Sidney Bastow Ltd to a small chain of private chemists owned by David Coleman; Timothy and his wife, however, retained ownership of the freehold of the premises at 50-50a North Street, and the current tenancy is actually assigned to Boots.

EASTGATE PHARMACY – 15 Eastgate Square

The pharmacy in Eastgate, familiar to Cicestrians as being run by George Bevis, has an earlier history. Records show that the first pharmacy on the site was initiated by Robert Wright in 1858, although the firm was passed to the Baker family – first Edward (in 1863), then Samuel (in 1871); and that Edward's prescription book covering the period 1863-1904 is still extant, together with an inventory of shop stock at 1875 .

Fig. 6. Shop sign for premises in time of the Baker family

In 1910 the pharmacy was purchased by George Frederick Bevis (1881-1938) who had qualified as a pharmacist in 1903. Two of his four children (from marriage with Miss Grace Stares) became qualified pharmacists: Mary (the eldest) who briefly took over the business on the death of her father, and who, on her own marriage to a local vet, George Begg, moved to Wickham, Hants; and George.

At the time of taking the business over from his sister (also in 1938), George Bevis, who had qualified as a pharmacist at Portsmouth in 1934, was working as a pharmacist in Brighton. He appreciated being able to spend more time in Chichester and after attending the meetings of the Chichester Amateur Operatic Society (founded in 1910), he fell in love with Rosalind Jeanne Turnbull, daughter of a former mayor and alderman of Chichester, George Turnbull of the Gentlemen's Outfitters of that name. Rosalind (it was her father who preferred 'Jeanne') had trained as a school dental nurse, but she had joined the Society in 1936. The shared interest in the Society throughout the war years cemented their relationship and they were married in 1946, George later

becoming Secretary 1948-56 and again in 1960, and Rosalind herself becoming a producer for the Society of Gilbert and Sullivan (succeeding the distinguished Margo Pink) from 1975 until her retirement in 1982.

George became a leading figure in local society – and became President of Chichester Camera Club, of Goodwood Golf Club (where he was a member for 48 years), and of Chichester Rotary. As hobbies, he delighted in growing carnations, and enjoyed wood

Fig. 7. Rosalind as a school dental nurse – a profession she pursued 1930-46 (The Schools Dental Service came into being as a consequence of the 1907 Education (Administrative Provisions) Act, which was the act that initiated the schools medical service

Fig. 8. The Eastgate Pharmacy – sporting the signs 'Dispensing Chemist' and Photographic Chemist', with George outside

carving. Despite these richly varied interests, he managed the pharmacy alone with a single assistant, but sold the business in 1981 to the Chotai Brothers, an Uckfield-based pharmacy chain trading under the Waremoss name and owning over 30 shops stretching mostly along the south coast but reaching also north to Luton, while retaining ownership of the building.

Today, the premises still exist on the historic site and the shop is managed by Mr Lloyd. George, himself, died 1 April 1989; but his widow, now in her nineties, still lives locally and I acknowledge here her kindness in permitting reproduction of images from her family album.

Fig. 9. George, in the middle, with his sister, Mary, and brother Reginald (1919) There were two sons from George's marriage, neither of whom wished to maintain the family tradition, arguing that chemists' hours were far too long for a good work/life balance; they both became solicitors and now discover they work much longer than they expected.

Since the sale of both these private chemists the Bevis shop and Bastows, there is at the present time in Chichester no privately-owned family pharmacy,[4] a situation that Timothy attributes to three causes: firstly, the progressive implementation of the 1964 Resale Prices Act, which, in prohibiting retail price maintenance, opened up competition in prices; secondly, the granting to doctors in rural areas (and Chichester counts as such) the right not just to prescribe, but also to dispense,[5] medicines to any patient who lives more than a certain distance (at present 1.6 kilometres) from the nearest retail pharmacy; and thirdly, the development of pharmacies in supermarkets and other large retail outlets.

This last, more recently, has been compounded by the onset of internet pharmacies, many routine products and medicines not requiring a prescription now being obtainable at the click of a button or two within the comfort of one's own home.

CODA

Mention was made above of the Boots Library, more accurately termed BBL – Boots Booklovers Library, which was initiated with a revolving stand in 1899 at the Pelham Street store in Nottingham. Within a year or two, the idea developed and by 1903 Boots had a library in 144 stores (50% of the then total), usually upstairs; and in the 1905 catalogue Jesse Boot emphasized that books were clean and gave 'assurances that potentially unsuitable books would be supplied as taste directed but not catalogued'. Such claims appealed to the clientele, mainly middle-class women – since the library required a subscription of 25 shillings a year, which conferred the right to borrow single books. The heyday of the scheme was the 1930s when 35 million books were handled each year, and even during WW2 over 1,000,000 books were being bought annually to add to and replace stock. The BBL in Chichester was not established at 11 South Street until 1936, although the store (No. 976) had  opened on 15th February 1917. The store moved to 62 South Street in 1965 (the current Bon Marché site), but not with its Library, which mostly had been closed by then across the country (*Courtesy Boots UK Archives*).

With grateful thanks to Timothy Bastow and Rosalind Bevis for assistance with this chapter.

---

[4] In a more recent development, many pharmacies within GP surgeries are now run by commercial firms – Lloyds, for instance, having almost 500 such venues

[5] In the period under discussion, there were other chemist shops in the city, but they were all branches of firms with a national presence: for instance, Savory and Moore at 64 South Street since about 1940 was founded in London in 1794 by a Thomas Paytherus, Thomas Savory joining in 1797 and establishing a partnership with Thomas Moore in 1806, the whole chain being taken over by Lloyds Pharmacy in 1992 – a firm that operates over 1600 pharmacies across Britain

Fig.10. Boots at 11 South Street, previously H. J. Horton – chemist and druggist from 1913, and from 1922 chemist and dental surgery

Fig. 11. Boots the Chemist, at 62 South Street

CONTRIBUTORS

Terry CARLYSLE, a recruit since moving to Chichester in 1998 to a band of enthusiastic local historians, has published *Chichester: the Castle in the Park* (New Chichester Paper Number 2 – Chichester Local History Society in association with University of Chichester, 2011).

Melissa COX, daughter of Nigel Purchase, lives locally and works in Chichester.

Alan H. J. GREEN is a local historian and author who was born and bred in Chichester. His published works on the history of his native city include *The Building of Georgian Chichester* (Phillimore, 2007); and he is chairman of both Chichester Conservation Area Advisory Committee and The Friends of St John's Chapel.

Ken GREEN, born in Chichester in 1932, was a pupil at Chichester High School where he later returned as a parent and then for several years as a governor. In 1986, following a lifelong interest, he founded the Chichester Local History Society; and is the author of several books about Chichester.

Sheila HALE, born, brought up, educated, worked, and married in the City, has always lived within five miles of the Market Cross – and consequently this 'stone' has gathered much Chichester 'moss'!

Frances LANSLEY has worked at West Sussex Record Office since 1994 and was appointed Searchroom Supervisor in 1999. She has lived in Chichester since 1988 and is interested in all aspects of local history.

Julie and Keith MASTERS are Cicestrians from birth and spent their working life in the City, Julie as a dance teacher before training at Bishop Otter College for work in a Primary School, and Keith as a clock and watchmaker, before appointment as a verger and sacristan at the cathedral; Keith previously contributed to Otter Memorial Paper Number 15, *A Jewel in Stone: Chichester Market Cross 1501-2001* (2001).

Susan MILLARD is the Searchroom Archivist at West Sussex Record Office. She was born and grew up in Chichester and attended Chichester High School for Girls. She is particularly interested in Oral History and has recorded the reminiscences of many local people. She is currently co-ordinating the Oving Memories Project.

Diana and Jim PAYNE were both born in Kent, Diana at Tonbridge, Jim at Dartford, but were to meet many years later. Jim's study and experience in the building industry led to appointment as a Technical Lecturer at Chichester College; and in the 1980s he continued study for a degree at Bishop Otter College (awarded in 1985), but also engaged actively in local politics and was twice Mayor of Chichester – 1990 and 1995. In contrast, Diana and her family had emigrated in 1952 to Australia for six years, and on her return she served and managed the family Jewellery Shop in Havant – where Keith Masters often visited to tend the clocks. Eventually, Diana and Jim met and married in Chichester.

David PRATT was born in Denmead, Hampshire in 1962 and studied at Portsmouth College of Art, University of Chichester, and The Prince's Drawing School, London. He now lives in Waterlooville. He is a member of Artel - an art group based in Chichester, where he has a studio. He specializes in drawing, but he has also created several works of eclectic sculpture which have been exhibited at the Cass Sculpture Park, Goodwood; at the Kijkduin Biennale, The Hague; and at Broomhill Sculpture Park in North Devon.

Stephen PRICE was born in Chichester and has lived most of his life either in or just south of the City. He started work at Hammick's Bookshop in East Street in the late 1980s, including three years as Manager, before entering publishing with Phillimore & Co. and, more recently, with The History Press.

Paddy WELSH is an Ulsterman who has lived in Chichester since 1950, working first as a reporter for local and national newspapers, radio, and television, and then as a public relations man for West Sussex Council and Southern Water. He is a past Chair of the Chichester Local History Society, but one of his main interests is walking and for twenty years he has led 250 walkers annually on the County Council`s sponsored walk of the 106-mile South Downs Way.

APPENDICES

APPENDIX 1

Occupants of shop premises

Occupants of some shop premises through the years. **Bold type** indicates businesses featured in *A Baker's Dozen*. T. G. Willis in his Book *Records of Chichester* (published in 1929) very helpfully recorded occupants of properties in East Street as he remembered them which we have 'borrowed'. Ten year gaps in the availability of Trade Directories and the fact that publication of them ceased in the mid-1970s means that readers will find many of their favourites missing from the list. We have striven for accuracy but some premises having been demolished with new buildings replacing them; others having been amalgamated; and in August 2011 a shortage of numbers on shop fronts, has led to some difficulties!

Eastgate Square

1	1665	Grocery founded by John Smith, thence through generations of the Hardham family
	1833	Henry John Hardham
	1860	**Sharp Garland, grocer and wine merchant**
		Sharp Archibald Garland, grocer and wine merchant
	1964	**Premises demolished and site redeveloped**
	2011	The Bazaar, cane furniture and fancy goods
4	1913	G. Hiscock, grocer
	1914	**Alfred Triggs, house furnishers and dealers**
	1936	**Alfred Triggs. Demolished 1936 and site redeveloped**
	2011	Look Fantastic, hairdresser
5	1913	G. H. Peskett, tailor
	1920	**Alfred Triggs, house furnishers and dealers.**
	1936	**Alfred Triggs. Demolished and site redeveloped**
	2011	Charlie Harper's, cafe
6	1913	A. H. Shotter, hand laundry
	1920	**Alfred Triggs, house furnishers and dealers**
	1936	**Alfred Triggs. Demolished and site redeveloped (Gaumont Cinema erected)**
	2011	Gordon House, flats
7	1913	H. Lee, carpenter & joiner
	1930	**Alfred Triggs, house furnishers and dealers**
	1936	**Alfred Triggs. Demolished and site redeveloped**
	2011	Carluccio's, authentic Italian restaurant
8	1913	W. Ord, Unicorn Inn
	2001	Chichester Observer Office
9	1843	Mr. H. Light, ironmonger and across the Sq.
	1913	**G. Pine, ironmonger**
	1928	**G. Pine, ironmonger moved business to the other premises**
	2011	Chichester Observer Office
??	**1928**	**G. Pine, ironmonger, in other premises Eastgate Square (not numbered)**
	1940	**G. Pine, ironmonger and post office**
	1990	**Business closed**
	2011	Fired Earth (13a)
14	1913	D. Stewart & Co., hatters and hosiers
	1930	Douglas Stewart, outfitters
	1940	Douglas Stewart, outfitters
	1950	Norman H. Fox, tailor
	1971	N. H. Fox, outfitter

	2011	**Eastgate Pharmacy**
15	1858	Robert Wright, The Eastgate Pharmacy
	1863	Edward Baker, The Eastgate Pharmacy
	1871	Samuel Baker, The Eastgate Pharmacy
	1910	**George Bevis, Snr. The Eastgate Pharmacy**
	1938	**George Bevis , Jnr. The Eastgate Pharmacy**
	1981	**Business sold to Waremoss, pharmacy chain**
	2011	Nisa Local, off licence and general store

East Street (*north side from the Cross*)

7 & 8	1869	Frederick Adames, ironmonger
	1871	Adames & Grant, ironmongers
	1880	Frederick Adames (late Adames & Grant), ironmonger
	1885	Adolphus Ballard
	1905	**T. E. Jay, ironmonger**
	1959	Sold to Tesco
	2011	HMV

15	**1906**	**William Kimbell, baker and confectioner**
15	**1908**	**(and bakehouse at 12 St. Martin's Street) William Kimbell, as above**
	1913	**William Kimbell, baker, confectioner and caterer**
		Kenrick, baker, confectioner and caterer
	1920	Wickham, baker confectioner and restaurateur (late Kenrick)
	(1929 - Willis)	Wickham, confectioner - formerly Long, chemist and stamp office; then W. Kimbell, confectioner; Kenrick
	1930	T. H. Fuller & Son, pastry cook, confectioners and caterers
	1932	**A. W. Rogers (Confectioners) Ltd**
	1962	Tip Top Bakeries
	1971	Acres the Bakers
	2011	Clinton's PLC, greetings cards ,wrapping paper, balloons etc.

(St. Martin's Street)

18	1891	Arthur Chitty, butcher
18	**1920**	**W. Goodger, butcher, game and poultry**
(1929 - Willis)		**Goodger & Son, butchers (formerly Warren, basket maker and turner; E. Lake; Chitty, butcher)**
	1933	**W. Goodger, butcher, game and poultry**
18/19	1936	J. Hepworth & Son Ltd., tailors
18/19/20	1939	J. Hepworth & Son. Ltd., tailors
16/17/18	1954	18 taken over by Marks & Spencer
19 & 20	1973	Still J. Hepworth & Son Ltd., tailors
	2011	Next, men's clothing

(Halifax - Alley to Oxmarket Art Centre)

22	(1929 - Willis) formerly Miss Stone, tobacconist	
23	" "	'The Red, White & Blue' public house
22/23	**1870**	**Byerley & Co., fishmonger and poulterers**
	1950	**Byerley & Co., (also had a second shop in South Street)**
	1954	Brighter Homes, Wallpapers
	1973	" " "
	2011	Field & Trek

26	**1881**	**Charges, drapers**
	1893	**Henry Morley Bishop, clothing store**
	1917	**Bishop's Clothing Stores Ltd**

	1994	**Business closed**
	2011	Orange, mobile phones

33   (1929 - Willis) W. C. Bridle, boot warehouse (formerly Miss Vine; Johnson; Harmsworth, fruiterer)

	1938	**Ford's (H. & S. Ford Ltd) boot and shoe repairers** (Established at 36b East Street between 1933 and 1936. Shown at No 33 in 1938.
	1969	**Ford's (H. & S. Ford Ltd) boot and shoe repairers**
	1973	Modern Shoe Repairs Ltd.
	2011	Hotel Chocolat, confectionery

34 & 35 **1833**   **A. J. Faith, watchmaker, silversmith, jeweller** (1823 G. Faith, watchmaker and clockmaker listed in High Street, Northend, Chichester - Somerstown)

	1978	
	or 1980	**Mr. Faith retired**
	2011	The Body Shop

36 & 37 **1861**   **Richard J. Jones & partner George J. Faith, drapers**

	1871	**George J. Faith, draper**
	1891	**George G. Faith, draper**

(1929 – Willis) Aylmore & Sons, grocers (formerly Loader, draper; Faith, draper; Aylmore and Lane)

	1954	36) Foyster & Sherborne, period and reproduction furniture shop
	1964	36) H. E. Foyster Ltd., period and reproduction furniture etc.
	1971	36) H. E. Foyster Ltd., period and reproduction furniture etc.
	2011	36) Oil & Vinegar; 37) White Wall, art gallery

(Little London)

39 **1880s**   **J. W. Moore founded business in Eastgate Square moved here at this date**

	(1929 -	
	Willis)	**Moore & Wingham, printers (formerly J. Mant, general cooper; Grover, ditto)**
	1945	**Moore & Tillyer, Stationers (Printing works in St. John's Street)**
	1996	**Stationer's shop closed**
	2003	**St. John's Street Printing Works closed**
	2011	Ryman's, stationers

50 **1946**   **Offord & Meynell, antiquarian bookshop and coffee bar**

	1976	**Business moved to 11 The Hornet as Meynell's Bookshop** (top floor of the Eastgate Gallery)

East Street (South side from Eastgate Square)

56 **1920**   **Parvins, costumiers**

(1929 – Willis) Madame Parvin, costumier (formerly C. Hoare, baker)

Post 1971 business closed

	2011	Harringtons Leather and Travel Goods

56a 1913-1971 Numerous tobacconists on ground floor, offices above

		David Paul Gallery extended to these premises
	1990	**Gallery closed**
	2011	Dartagnan, clothing for men

57   1913   Bacon & Co., hosiers etc.

	1920	H. J. Vale, high class pastry cook & confectioner

(1929 – Willis) Orchard Fruit Stores (formerly: Giles, butcher; C. T.Muggeridge, house furnisher; Hart, gunsmith)

	1929	**George Bunn (Orchard Fruit Stores), fruiterer and greengrocer**

		(started business at 15 & 16 George Street 1920)

      1964   **Business closed**
      1964   H. Wain & Sons, fruiterers
      1968   Melbray, fruiterers
      1973   Quartons, fruiterers
      2011   Caffe Nero

60   1913   London & County Stores (manager H. Ballard)
      1920   Guy Dental Institute, W. H. Griffin
      (1929 Willis) Guy's Dental Institute (formerly Pillow & Son, music sellers; White's Oil and
            Colour Stores)
      1930   A. J. O'Flananagan, dentist
      1950   Peter Boutwood, dental surgeon; John McStea, chiropodist
      1964   **Penney & Son (Chichester) Ltd., dress fabrics, household linens and
            furnishing fabrics etc.**
      post 1973 **Business closed**
      2011   Champneys, spa

66   (1929 – Willis) Longlands, outfitters (formerly: H. Prior, outfitter; Fred Longlands)
66a   (1929 – Willis) Private House
66 & 66a **1931**   **J. Baker & Co. Ltd., outfitter**
      1973   Morrelli's Cafe
66 & 66a 2011   Cheltenham & Gloucester Building Society

68   (1929 – Willis) **Mrs. W. H. Gardiner, cycle agent** (formerly: Young, dyers; F. Chitty,
            mineral water works; Malby, photographers; Bardon, photographers)
            Gardiners, cycle agents in these premises prior to 1913
      1960s (early) business closed
      1968   Chapman's Laundry
      1971   Chapman's Laundry, receiving office
      2011   3 Store, mobile phones

71   **1901**   **C. J. Elphick, pork butcher**
      (1929 – Willis) C. F. Elphick, pork butcher (formerly: William Gale, toy merchant; Clinch;
            Mant, pork butcher)
      1973   **C. J. Elphick Ltd**
71 & 72 2011   Monsoon, ladies clothing

76   **1868**   **Doman's Cheap Drapery Business** (founded by William Doman)
      1890   **second linen shop opened at 24 North Street**
      (1929 – Willis) **Doman & Son, drapers** (formerly: Robert Smith, tailor)
77   (1929 – Willis) Fletcher Ltd., butchers. (formerly: Smith, tailor)
76 & 77 **1968**   **Domans Furnishings Ltd., soft furnishings and linens**
      1974   "   "   " **moved to 38-40 The Hornet (closed 1980)**
      2011   Clarks, shoe retailers

78   1913   A. E. Cowley, baker, confectioner and restaurateur
      (1929 – Willis) G. L. Smith, confectioner (formerly Finch; Wright; Richardson; F. Hardham;
            A.B.C.; Cowley)
      1920   **Tudor Café, proprietor G. L. Smith**
      1971   **Business closed**
      1971   Singer Sewing Machine Company
      2011   Early Learning Centre

(North Pallant)

81 & 82 **1820s**   **Halsted & Sons, ironmongers (foundry in Baffin's Lane – now a car park)**
      (1929 – Willis) **Halsted & Son** (formerly C. Critchell and Edward Critchell, bootmakers)

	1936	**Business closed**

81 & 82 1938   **81** Misses M. & M. Holliday, café A. Lewis & Co. (Westminster) Ltd, tobac; & Ed. J. H. Smith, hairdresser**. 82** Masters & Co. (Clothiers) Ltd., outfitters)

        1954   **81** The Pallant Tea Rooms, proprietors Major & Mrs. Ansell. A. Lewis & Co. (Westminster) Ltd, tobacconist, and Edward J. H. Smith, hairdresser**. 82** Masters & Co. (Clothiers) Ltd., outfitters

        1964   Dragon Spring Chinese Restaurant. (81 A. Lewis & Co. (Westminster) Ltd. 82 John Temple Ltd., tailors

        1968   As above

        1973   As above

81   2011   Pia, jewellery

82   2011   CC, ladies clothing

83   **c. 1899- 1903 Edward Henry Lewis took over the business from Thomas Henry Couch**

        1913   **E. H. Lewis, clockmaker**

        (1929 - Willis) Lewis & Sons, jewellers (formerly Wilmshurst & Son, jewellers; Crouch)

        1933   **E. H. Lewis & Sons Ltd., jewellers**

        1950   **E. H. Lewis & Sons (R.L. Austen Ltd.) jewellers**

        1968   **R. L. Austen Ltd., had moved to 75 North Street**

83   2011   Viyella

84   **1899**   **Alfred Ernest Reynolds, hatter and hosier**

        (1929 – Willis) Reynolds, hosier (formerly Hardham, confectioner)

        1930   **Guy Reynolds, gents. outfitter** (between 1933 & 1936 business moved to 77 North Street)

        1936   Mac Fisheries Ltd., fishmongers

        1973   Mac Fisheries Ltd., fishmongers

        2011   Fat Face, clothing

87   1866   Thomas Kimbell, grocer, 13 George Street, Somerstown

        1899   **Thomas Kimbell, East Street and George Street**

        1901   David Kimbell, butcher, 45 & 46 George Street

        1913   **Kimbell & Sons, butcher and provision merchant**

        (1929 – Willis) Kimbell & Sons, pork butchers (formerly: Gates, butcher; Inkson, pork butcher; then sundry; Vick, pork butcher)

        1968   **Premises vacant**

        1969   Baxters, butchers

        1973   Premises not listed

        2011   Lush, fresh handmade cosmetics

Northgate

16   1899   Charles Petto in business at 10 Whyke Lane

        1913   J. Newman, curio dealer

        1920   **H. J. Petto, boot and shoe repairer** (Charles Petto, 10 Whyke Lane)

        1996   **Last family shoemaker retired**

        2011   The Photographic Lounge

North Street: *(West side from the Cross)*

9   1786   John Phillipson first chemist recorded on this site and subsequently until

        1903   **Sidney Bastow, pharmaceutical & photographic chemist**

        1985   **Business moved to new premises at 50 Northgate**

        2011   British Bookshops (W.H. Smith, stationers)

13   **1909**   **A. Andrews, cycle dealer, sports depot, electrical goods and motor accessories**

        1972   **Business closed**

        1973   Rediffusion Television Rental

        2011   Starbucks Coffee Company

19	1899	Joseph R. Hobbs, baker, and 86 North Street (formerly Cavendish Street)
	1945	**A. E. Spurrier & Son , baker & confectioner (and 70/71 South Street)**
	1958	**A. E. Spurrier & Son, baker & confectioner, sold 19 North Street**
	1964	Posner Gowns Ltd., ladies outfitters
	1971	Posner Gowns Ltd., ladies outfitters
	2011	Holland & Barrett, health foods
21	1736	Mary & William Pannell, mealman
	1913	E. Moore, West Sussex Stores, outfitters and house furnishers (pawnbroking and second hand goods, 20 & 21 Chapel Street)
	1938	Egbert Moore Ltd., outfitters
	1939	**Laurie Kimbell, baker, confectioner & restaurateur**
	1954	**Business closed**
	1954	John Perring, house furnisher
	2011	Marks & Spencer
24	**1890**	**Doman Furnishing Ltd., drapers**
	1949	**Doman's Fashions Ltd., ladies outfitters and costumiers**
	1969	**Business closed**
	1971	Gabicat, ladies outfitters
	1973	As above
	2011	Britannia Building Society
26	1913	Premises unoccupied
	1920	C. Harnett, Cycle Agent
	1930	Harry Hewitt, Cycle Agent
	1933	**Boyce & Chitty, cycle agents**
	1938	**Boyce & Chitty, wireless dealers**
	1950	**Chitty Bros. Ltd., wireless dealers**
	1964	**Premises unoccupied – Chitty Bros. Ltd. removed to 28 North Street**
	1968	Wimpy Bar
	2011	Toni & Guy, hairdressers

(Crane Street)

28	1933	John West, antique dealer
	1936	John West, antique dealer; Rene (Miss R. Baker) ladies hairdresser
	1950	John West, antique dealer: Patricia (A. & P. Wimhurst), ladies hairdressers
	1964	**Chitty Bros., cycle dealers, repairers, electrical goods and contractors, bee keeping equipment**
	1980s	**Business closed**
		Fludes Carpets
	2011	Chantry House, oak and rugs
31	1913	H. Austin Storry Ltd., pianoforte and music warehouse
	1920	Dr. D. Ewart
	1930	Mervyn Farwell
	1933-1954	Miss C.I.R. Heriot
	1956	**Arthur Purchase & Son, wine merchant**
	2011	Amelie and Friends, restaurant, (south side)
	2011	Strutt & Parker, estate agents (north side)
32	1913	Dr. D. Ewart
	1920	Children's Welfare Centre – Nurse Scott
	1930	**Arthur Purchase & Son, wine and spirit merchant**
	1956	**Business removed to 31 North Street**
	1964	Cresta Couture, ladies fashion specialists

	2011	Laura Ashley
39	**1857**	**J. H. Smurthwaite, decorators merchant**
	1980	C. Brewer & Sons, decorators merchants
	1987	C. Brewer & Sons removed to new premises
	2011	Basler, ladies' fashions
45	1913	W. H. Osborn, plumber
	1920	W. H. Osborn, builder
	1930	Harry Osborn, architect
	1940	Harry Osborn, architect
	1949	**Jupp & Laker, ironmongers**
	1958	**Business closed**
	1958	Northgate Florists (Margaret Sharp), florists and post office
	1973	Northgate florists still listed
	2011	Meritz, sports, ski, snowboard, etc.
47	1913	W. Stoner, 'Foresters Arms' public house
	1920	F. G. Hart, 'Foresters' Arms'. public house
	1930	Mrs. A. Young, confectioner
	1936	**Mickey's, confectioner, tobacconist & provision merchant (Michael Guarnaccio)**
	1983	**Death of Michael Guarnaccio**
	1983	Orchard Greengrocer
	2011	Orchard Tea Rooms
49	1913	A. H. Watts, antique furniture dealer
	1920	F. Somers
	1933	C. H. Trussler, engineer
	1936	**Joseph T. Binns, chemist**
	1973	**Binns Chemist (proprietor Ivor Hughes)**
	19??	Dry Cleaners
	2011	Grants Quality Dry Cleaner

North Street *(East side from Northgate)*

50	1913	W. Carpenter, fried fish merchant
	1930	Mrs. Kate Day, fish restaurant
	1938	David Day, fish restaurant
	1964	Seafare (Brighton) Ltd., fish restaurant
	1973	As above
	1985	**Sidney Bastow, chemists**
		Sold business but not the property
	2011	Boots Pharmacy
50a	**1985**	**Bastows Classics, specialist music department**
	2011	**Bastows Classics**
67	1911	Census shows North House Private Hotel (manageress Hilda Purchase)
	1935	Hotel demolished
	1936	**North House erected on site.**
	1940	No 1 Arthur Young Ltd., butchers
	1959	**No 1 Prior & Sons, fruiter & greengrocer**
	1989	**Business closed**
	2011	No 1 The Coln Gallery, artists materials
68	1913	A. G. Harrington, dental surgeon
	1920	V. Spill, dental surgeon
	1930	Alex James Roberts, dental surgeon

	1959	**Ray's Hardware, hardware merchant and ironmonger (Ray Chatfield)**
	1969	**Business transferred to Mr. D. G. Jeffery**
	1980	**Business closed**
	2011	Coral, the bookmaker
70	1850's	Thomas Gadd, grocer (James Hopkins, 36 West Street, apprenticed to him)
	1867	Edward Gadd, grocer
	1899	Edward John Gadd, grocer, provision & wine & spirit merchant
	1913	J. Long, furniture store
	1920	Unoccupied
	1930	Mrs. M. F. Kendall, furniture dealer
	1940	Sussex Cake Co. Ltd.
	1950	John Atkins Ltd., bakers
	1964	F. W. Mitchell, Ltd., bakers
	1971	F. W. Mitchell Ltd., bakers
	2011	Jacques Vert, ladies fashions
71	1913	**C. A. Hennings, bootmaker and repairer, and leather dealer**
	1954	**Premises unoccupied**
	1964	Andrew McDowall, ladies' outfitters (and no. 72)
	2011	Phones 4U, mobile phones
72	1913	Mrs. A. Baber, confectioner
	1930	**Ernest Edward Voke, fruiterer (1920 Voke & Son, fruiterers at no. 77)**
	1964	Andrew McDowall, ladies' outfitters
	2011	Phones 4U, mobile phones

(Lion Street)

73	1881	**H. Penney & Co. Ltd., draper, ladies' outfitters. milliner and household linens**
	1960s	**moved to smaller premises at 60 East Street in early 60s. Closed in 1973**
	1964	Currys Ltd., cycles, radios, t.v. and electrical goods
	2011	Dorothy Perkins, ladies' outfitters
75	1913	Premises unoccupied
	1920	F. Janeece, confectioner
	1930	H. H. Ludlow, Wholesale and Retail leather merchant
	1964	As above
	1968	**R. L. Austen Ltd., jeweller (had moved from 83 East Street)**
	2011	**R. L. Austen Ltd., jeweller**
77	1913	J. D. Cossey, family chemist
	1920	**Voke & Son, fruiterers**
	1930	Albert Inkpen, fruiterer
	1936	**Guy Reynolds, hatter, tailor, hosier, glover etc. (formerly 87 East Street)**
	1987	**Business closed**
		Beneton
	2011	Boots the Opticians
78	1899	Charles Rees, linen draper
	1913	**G. A. Geering, draper and haberdasher**
	1920	**G. A. Geering, draper and milliner**
	1930	**G. A. Geering, draper & milliner**
	1953	**William Clark & Sons, decorators merchants**
	1967	**Taken over by R. R. Perry & Sons**
	1975	**Business moved to Adelaide Road**
	2011	Macari's Coffee Shop

(Crooked 'S' (Shambles Alley)

79	1899	**John Voke, baker and confectioner (also at 47 The Hornet)**
	1901	**Kate Voke, confectioner**
	1913	T. E. Beacham, confectioner
	1920	M. H. Woolley, confectioner
	1930	**G. A. Geering, draper & milliner**
	1973	**Geerings (Chichester) Ltd., departmental store**
	2011	Between the Lines, gifts and cards
80	1913	W. C. Bowles, Wheatsheaf Hotel
	1920	**G. A. Geering, draper & milliner**
	1930	**G. A. Geering, draper & milliner**
	1973	**Geerings (Chichester) Ltd., departmental store**
	2011	Robert Dyas, electrical and household goods
81	**1861**	**Census shows George Howard, master butcher**
	1881	**Census shows Charlie Howard as a butcher, with widowed mother**
	1929	**Business sold but name and Royal Warrant continued in use until 1964**
	1968	Cheltenham & Gloucester Building Society
	2011	Swallow Bakery

(St. Olave's Church)

Market House (The Buttermarket)

	1935	**Miss Agnes M. Cripps, fishmonger**
	1976	**No. 3 Miss Cripps died and business ceased**
	1953	**No.21 Hoopers of Chichester, florists**
	1962	**Opened a second shop at 14 South Street**
	1984	**Business closed**
	1957	**No.2 Prior & Sons, butchers**
	1989	**Business closed**

84	**1899**	**Henry Denyer, draper**
	1954	**Henry Denyer, draper**
	1964	**Not in directory**
	1968	Top Rank Home & Leisure Service
	1971	Granada Robinson, television rentals
	2011	Accessorize, ladies accessories
85	**1913**	**Henry Turner & Sons, boot maker, repairer & and retail shoe shop (workshop Franklin Place)**
	1964	**Business sold to Messrs. Jones, shoe retailers**
	2011	Jones, shoe retailer
86	**1899**	**Joseph Richard Hobbs, confectioner and 19 North Street, baker** (formerly in Cavendish Street)
86 and 87	2011	Hotter shoes

Southgate *(West side)*

13	**1899**	**Francis Kimbell, baker and confectioner**
	1913	H. Venner, baker & confectioner
	1930	Albert Brown, baker
	1939	Frederick Charles Glue, baker
	1950	Devonia Bakery (J. Pratt)
	1954	Devonia Bakery (C. J. Batty)

	1964	Coffee Mill, coffee house
	1971	Coffee Mill, coffee house

Southgate *(east side)*

31	1905	**Charles C. Allen, watchmaker**
	1913	H. T. Bentley, hairdresser
	1920	C. Jeffries, hairdresser
	1954	C. Jeffries, hairdresser
	1964	Botterill & Co., coal merchants
	1971	Byng's Luxury Coaches Ltd.
	1973	Premises not listed
	2011	Lucky House, Peking & Cantonese Cuisine, take away

32a	1930	**Websters, nurserymen, seedsmen & florists (Nursery in Market Avenue)**
	1971	**Still listed as above**
	1972	**Business closed**
	1973	Premises not listed.**Premises used for a time as second Chichester Bookshop**
	2011	Now 33? Gemini, hairdresser

39	1964	Premises unoccupied
	1968	**The Chichester Bookshop (proprietor George Thompson)**
	1970s	**The Chichester Bookshop Ltd. (when John Dent became a partner)**
		second-hand and antiquarian bookshop
	1994	**John Dent's Bookshop**
	1997	Chichester Bookshop (Nick Howell, proprietor)
	2008	Chichester Bookshop (proprietors Chris and Carol Lowndes) closed
	2011	High House, financial services

South Street *(West side from the Cross)*

1/2	1851	George Glover, master stationer (on his later retirement, business taken over by his daughter, Mary Ann Glover
	1871	**W. H. Barrett, bookseller and stationer**
	1923	**Death of W. H. Barrett** (business contd under the same name, run by Ernest H. Thompson who in 1890 had married Nelly Victoria Barrett, daughter)
	1960	**Premises of W. H. Barrett bought by the City Council and later demolished**
	2011	Russell & Bromley, shoe retailers, in premises later erected on part of the site

3 & 4	1930	**Charles Shippam, pork butcher and provision merchant**
	1954	**as above**
3	1964	Russell & Bromley Ltd, shoe retailers
	1971	as above
	2011	as above
4	1964	Milletts (Sutton) Ltd., outfitters
	1971	as above
	2011	as above

4 & 5	1913	**Charles Shippam, pork butcher and provision merchant**
	1920	**as above**
	2011	Quba & Co, clothing

8	1913	J. Tisdall, gun maker
	1920	as above
	1930	**C. C. Allen & Son, jewellers**
	1940	**as above**
	1950	F. M. Barber Ltd, fishmongers
	1964	Tip Top Bakeries

	1968	Steyning & Sussex County Building Society
	1971	as above
	2011	Timpson, boot and shoe repairs, keys cut, house signs
9/10	1845	Henry Gadd, wholesale and retail draper (his brother Thomas was a grocer)
	1862	**Michael Turnbull acquired the business from Mr Gadd**
	1881	**G. M. Turnbull, joined his father in drapery business**
	1890	**Took Alfred Sykes into partnership in drapery business.** Partnership dissolved during World War 1. G. M. Turnbull continued with his outfitters & hosiery business at 62 and 63 South Street
	1919	**Alfred Sykes & Son Ltd., clothing, fabrics and millinery. Son, Leonard joined the business**
	1946	**Alfred Sykes & Son Ltd. Peter Sykes joined the business**
	1967	**Alfred Sykes & Son Ltd. Business taken over by Peter Sykes**
	1983	**Alfred Sykes & Son Ltd. Peter Sykes retired.**
	1983	**Austin-Sykes (taken over by Alan Austin)**
	1989	**Austin-Sykes did not renew lease on premises.** (Moved to temp. premises in The Old Theatre, South Street, and subsequently to St. Pancras. Closed 2004)
9	2011	Rohde, shoe retailers)
10	2011	Sahara, clothing
12	1913	The Crown, public house
	1920	The Crown, public house
	1930	**Henry Wakeford, florist**
	1954	**Henry Wakeford, florist**
	1958	**G. W. Syrett, fruiterer** (formerly Manager for Spurriers)
	1968	H. Beresford, milliner
	1973	Premises vacant
	2011	Timothy Roe Fine Jewellery Ltd.
14	1913	Mrs. J. Rose, milliner
	1920	**Charge & Co. drapers (and 1 South Street)**
	1962	**Hoopers of Chichester, florists (and 21 The Buttermarket)**
	1980s	**Closed**
	2011	East Ltd., ladies fashions
19	1913	F. M. Barber (Fish) Ltd., fishmongers
	1950	**Byerley & Co., fishmonger and poulterers (22/23 East Street formerly)**
	1984	**Sold to Hoopers of Portsmouth**
	1998	**Hoopers closed**
	2011	White Stuff Ltd.
19a	1913	Madame H. Maye, costumier
	1930	Sybille, costumier
	1954	Skinner & Rea Ltd., travel agents
	1960	**S. J. Linkins, luggage and handbags (see also 22 South Street)**
	1980s(late)	**Business closed**
	2011	Mr. Simms Olde Sweet Shoppe, confectioner
21	**1913**	**V. C. Weston, fruiterer**
	1930	**V. C. Weston & Son, fruiterer**
	1940	**The City Fruit Stores (V. C. Weston & Sons proprietors) fruiterers**
	1975	**Business closed**
	2011	Musto Ltd., clothing
22	1760	Mr. Miller, saddler and harness maker. William Gambling apprenticed to Mr. Miller later taking over the business, and thence to his son, Robert Gambling 1920

Robert Gambling, harness maker

	1922	**S. J. Linkins, saddler**
	1930	**S. J. Linkins, sports outfitter**
	1960	**S. J. Linkins, sports outfitter and leather goods. H. J. Middleton, Managing Director expanded business and opened 19a South Street**
	1980s	**(late) Business closed**
	2011	Chesca

(Canon Lane)

24	1913	Miss F. Osmond
	1930	**Miss F. Osmond (24a Robert Allen, watchmaker)**
	1933	**Robert Allen, watchmaker**
	1950	Robert Allen (proprietors W. & S.A. Darby) watchmakers
	1964	Robert Allen, (proprietors W. & S.A.. Darby) watchmaker
	1968	**Wessex Bookshop, booksellers**
	1980s	**Wessex Bookshop, booksellers**
	2011	Cath Kidston

25	1913	R. Walter, confectioner
	1920	**Hooper & Son, florists and fruiterers (and no. 26)**
	1930	George H. Martin, antique dealer
	1950	Malcolm McNeille (Sussex) Ltd., photographers (and no. 26)
	1954	Malcolm McNeille (Sussex) Ltd., photographers (and no. 26)
	1964	Property not listed
	1971	Property not listed
	2011	Store Twenty One, clothing

26	**1913**	**Hooper & Son, florists and fruiterers**
	1920	**Hooper & Son, florists and fruiterers**
	1930	Malcolm McNeille & Co., photographers
	1950	Malcolm McNeille (Sussex) Ltd., photographers (and no. 25)
	1954	Malcolm McNeille (Sussex) Ltd., photographers (and no. 25)
	1964	Wendovers, (Chichester) Ltd. house furnishers
	1968	Wendovers (Chichester) Ltd. house furnishers
	1973	Wendovers (Chichester) Ltd. house furnishers
	2011	Store Twenty One, clothing

27	1913	J. Turner & Son, grocers
	1930	**Hooper's & Son, fruiterers**
	1950	**Hooper's, florists**
	1954	**Property not listed**
	1964	J. M. Footwear Ltd. shoe dealers
	1968	Manda, shoe dealers
	1971	The Blue Orchid, Restaurant
	1973	The Blue Orchid, Restaurant
	2011	Pizza Express (Restaurants) Ltd.

30	1913	F. Chitty, mineral water manufacturer (and 31)
	1927	**Russell Hillsdon, gun maker and athletic outfitter**
	1950	**Russell Hillsdon, sports outfitter**
	1954	Porosan Plastics Ltd., plastic manufacturers
	1954	Polyestol Ltd. surgical bandage manufactures
	1954	Walter E. Engel, consulting chemist
	1969-1973	Leslie's Hairdressers
	2011	Tourist Information Office

South Street *(East side from Southgate)*

46	1913	C. J. & W.H. Sayers, upholsterers
	1930	A. & G. Wimhurst Ltd. general merchants
	1938	A. & G. Wimhurst Ltd., wholesale grocers, confectioners, fruiterers & authorised potato merchants
	1950	Property not listed
	1954	**Russell Hillsdon, sports outfitter**
	1984	**Russell Hillsdon, sports outfitters closed**
		Lakeland Plastics, kitchen & household goods
	2011	L. J's for Jeans; upstairs The Big Man Shop

49	1913	J. Walker & Son, tailors
	1920	**T. Lummus, electrical engineer**
	1930	**Thomas F. Lummus, wireless engineer**
	1954	**Thomas F. Lummus, electrical engineer**
	1964	**Willards Electrical Services Ltd. (props: H.E.Willard & Son; T.E. Lummus)**
	1971	**As above**
	1987	**Shop closed – business moved to the Terminus Road Industrial Estate**
	2011	Cancer Research U.K.

59	1913	**C.C. Allen, watchmaker & jeweller**
57, 58 & 59	1920	**C.C. Allen, watchmaker & jeweller**
	1930	**C. C. Allen & Son, watchmakers**
	1980s	**Business sold**
57 & 58	2011	Rowlands of Bath, Clothing
59	2011	Past Times fancy goods

(West Pallant)

62	**1899**	**G. M. Turnbull, outfitter and hosier**
62 & 63	**1913**	**G. M. Turnbull, outfitter and hosier**
	1954	**G. M. Turnbull, gents outfitter**
	1964	**Premises not listed**
	1968	Boots Cash Chemists (Southern) Ltd.
	1971	Timothy Whites Ltd. chemist
		TSB Bank
	2011	Bon Marche, ladies clothing

63	**1851**	**Charges, drapers**
	2011	Bon Marche, as above

(Cooper Street)

65	1913	**J. D. Webster, florist**
	1920	Curry & Co. cycle agents
	1930	Curry's Ltd. cycle agents
	1954	Curry's Ltd. cycle agents
	1964	John Boyes (Stores) Ltd. house furnishers
	1971	John Boyes (Stores) Ltd. house furnishers
	2011	Barnardo's Charity Shop

70/71	1899	Charles Richardson, baker and confectioner
	1913	Joseph R. Hobbs, J.P., baker (and 19 North Street)
	1940	Joseph R. Hobbs, J.P., baker (and 19 North Street)
	1945	**A. E. Spurrier & Son, bakers at both addresses**
	1958	**A. E. Spurrier & Son, bakers – at this address only**
	1979	**A. E. Spurrier & Son, bakers**
	1980	Sussex Building Society
71	2011	Perfect Timing, clocks and watches

72/73	**1862**	**Alfred Dunn, draper**
	1913	**Dunn & Son (Drapers, Chichester) Ltd (Cheap Drapery Bazaar)**
	1954	**Dunn & Son (Drapers, Chichester) Ltd.**
	1964	Stead & Simpson Ltd. shoe retailers
	1973	Stead & Simpson Ltd. shoe retailers
73	2011	Stead & Simpson Ltd. shoe retailers
72	2011	Vision Express, opticians
74/75	**1913**	**Charge & Co., linen draper, silk mercer and clothier** (formerly at no. 1)
	1922	**Charge & Co.**
	1968	**Premises sold to Midland Bank**
	2011	HSBC Bank

St. John's Street *(off south side of East Street)*

	1960	**David Paul Gallery, art dealers and picture framers (proprietors Constance & Shirley Fox & David Goodman)**
	1990	**Gallery closed**
	2011	Licensed Café and take away (see also 56a East Street)
	1950	**Moore & Tillyer Ltd. printers, bookbinders, machine rulers and account book makers (office and works)**
	2003	**Printing Works closed**
	2011	Greyfriars, flats

St. Martin's Square

12a	**1958**	**The Practical Upholsterers Ltd.**
	1991	**Moved to Walberton. (1997 moved to premises in Pound Farm Road, Chichester where they remain in 2011)**

St. Pancras *(off Eastgate Square)*

	1824	William and John Leng listed as cabinet makers at Northgate and Eastgate
	1867	John & William Leng, cabinet makers at Northgate and Eastgate
1	**1899**	**John Leng & Sons, cabinet makers and upholsterers**
	1913	**J. Leng & Son, upholsterers and cabinet makers (and at 156 St. Pancras)**
	1930	**Jn. Leng & Sons, furniture dealers (and 156)**
1 & 2	**1950**	**Jn. Leng & Sons (Chichester) Ltd. house furnishers (not at 156)**
	1964	**Jn. Leng & Sons (Chichester) Ltd. house furnishers**
	1968	Farr's Depositories Ltd. removal contractors
	1971	Farr's Depositories Ltd. **and Dora Sharpe (Bennetts) florist**
	20??	St. Wilfrid's Hospice Shop
	2011	Cloth Kits, printed clothing kits
14	**1874**	**Francis Kimbell, grocer**
	1880	**Francis Kimbell, baker and corn dealer**
	1913	D. Napper, baker & confectioner
	1927	Ernest Frederick Tupper, shopkeeper
	1933	Ernest Charles Taulbut, baker
	1950	Jn. Alan Furneaux, baker
	1964	Mrs. M. Furneaux, baker
	1973	Ye Olde Bakery
		Mary Morris & Pozzi, bakery
	2011	India Gate, restaurant

(New Park Road; Alexandra Road; Adelaide Road)

77	1954	A. J. Cuddington & Co. Ltd., baby carriage dealers
156	1913	John Leng & Son, upholsterers and cabinet makers
	1950	Hoad & Holder, cycle agents and electrical services
	1971	As above
	1973	Business closed
	1973	Adcocks Car radio and accessory Centre
	2011	Big Wave Productions Ltd., television, video and radio services

South Pallant

10	1952	The Practical Upholsterers Farrs Ltd
	1953	The Practical Upholsterers Ltd (having taken over top floor)
	1958	Moved to 12a St. Martin's Square

Spitalfield Lane

43	1913	Cliffie George Stenning, cycle dealer and repairer
	2005	Business closed
	2011	Reynolds. Funeral Director

The Hornet

6	1899	John Voke, baker & confectioner (formerly 47 - premises renumbered, in the 1930s) & at 79 North Street
	1901	John Voke, baker & confectioner (daughter Kate running 79 North Street shop)
	1907	Henry John Voke, baker, confectioner and caterer opened a tea garden at the back of their shop
	1940	Business closed
	2011	Goodrowes, agricultural machinery
11	1968	D. G. Jeffery (Chichester) Ltd. builder, contractor etc.
	1971	Premises unoccupied
	1971	The Eastgate Gallery, art gallery
	1976	also, first floor, Meynell's Bookshop, antiquarian and second hand books (moved from 50 East Street)
	1985	Meynell's Bookshop closed
	1987	Opening of renovated and extended Eastgate Gallery
	????	Business closed
	2011	Buzby & Blue, hairdressers
21		Henry George Ferry, bootmaker and repairer
	1960	Erban Kazimierz, son-in-law of Mr. Ferry, had been working with him and took over the business on Mr. Ferry's death, boot maker and repairer
	1971	As above
	1985	Business closed
	2011	Beyond the Fringe, vintage and retro clothing
36	1899	Lewis Seward, saddler and harness maker
	1922	Percy H. Seward, saddler
	1971	Percy H. Seward, saddler and fishing tackle
	1985	Business closed
	2011	Perfect Pizza

38-40	1974	**Purpose built shop for Doman's Furnishings Ltd.**
	1980	**Business closed**
	2011	Country Style Interiors
42	1936	**William Goodger, butcher (formerly had premises in West Street and East Street)**
	????	**Business closed**
	2011	The Charcoal Grill
108	1940	**William J. Voke, baker**
	1954	**William J. Voke, baker**
	1964	Planet Models & Handicrafts
	1973	As above
	2011	Light & Shade Interiors
124	1900s	Father of C. H. Noyce, boot and shoe repairer already at these premises (originally at 130 The Hornet – wooden hut, currently not occupied)
	1917	C. H. Noyce joined his father
	1970s	(early) business closed. Mr. Noyce died in 1986
	2011	Beauteek, holistic beauty treatments

West Street (north side)

2	1898	**(formerly West Ashling) W. Goodger, butcher (later had premises in East Street and The Hornet)**
	1922	**Had moved to 18 East Street**
	1969	Pride & Joy Ltd., baby wool
	1973	Freckles, ladies wear
	2011	Moda In Pelle, footwear
18	1933	**Tower Café, premises owned by Morants, business owned by the Smith brothers who also had Tudor Café, East Street**
	1955	**Closed when Morants Department Store was sold to Army & Navy. (Tudor Café still operating in 1954 but not listed in 1964)**
	2011	House of Fraser, department store
36	1857	**James Hopkins, grocer**
	1913	**Hopkins & Son, grocers**
	1930	**J. W. Hopkins & Son, grocers**
	1961	**Premises demolished by WSCC for road widening scheme**

My grateful thanks to Olive Glover and Betty Randall, who helped so much by sharing their memories of Chichester with me. SH

APPENDIX 2
ILLUSTRATION CREDITS

All the whole page illustrations, including that of the unicycle rider (who represents the subjects of the thirteen chapters in *A Baker's Dozen*) have been specially drawn by David Pratt – with 'period' features, including smoking whilst mowing! All other illustrations are acknowledged below by chapter followed by a Figure number, e.g.. Fig. 5.3 is the labelled detail of the Purchase family and staff in Nigel Purchase's painting of North Street which features in Chapter 5, 'Liquid Refreshment'.

1.1 Sheila Hale; 1.2 West Sussex Record Office/Paul Foster; 1.3 West Sussex Record Office; 1.4 Carole Bisogni; 1.5 Carole Bisogni; 1.6 Chichester Camera Club/Chichester District Museum; 1.7 Chichester Camera Club/Chichester District Museum; 1.8 C.M. Scutt; 1.9 C.M. Scutt; 1.10 Ken Green; 1.11 Ken Green; 1.12 West Sussex Record Office 1.13 Bernard Price literature

2.1.Ken Green literature; 2.2 Bernard Price literature; 2.3 Chichester City Council; 2.4 Chichester Camera Club/Chichester District Museum; 2.5 Victor Goodeve; 2.6 AHJ Green Collection; 2.7 Terry Carlysle; 2.8 Alan H. J. Green Collection; 2.9 Sheila Hale; 2.10 John Templeton; 2.11 Bernard Price Literature; 2.12 John Hooper; 2.13 Mary Prior; 2.14 John Shippam; 2.15 Ray Elderton, Ingleburn, Australia

3.1 Anon.; 3.2 Ken Green; 3.3 Ken Green; 3.4 Chichester Camea Club/Chichester District Museum; 3.5 Sheila Hale/Chichester Directory; 3.6 Chichester Camera Club/Chichester District Museum; 3.7 Ken Green; 3.8 Mary Prior; 3.9 Mary Prior; 3.10 Ken Green/Steve Griffith literature; 3.11 Gaynor Williams; 3.12 Price Family Archive; 3.13 Chichester Camera Club/Chichester District Museum; 3.14 Jim Weston; 3.15 Jim Weston

4.1 M. Woodier; 4.2 Chichester Observer (marking the 75th anniversary of the firm); 4.3 Ken Green; 4.4 Noyce Family; 4.5 Pamela Gilbert; 4.6 Ken Green; 4.7 Pat Combes; 4.8 Chichester District Museum; 4.9 Ken Green; 4. 10 John Seward; 4.11 Bernard Price literature; 4.12 Tandy Leather (United States of America)

5.1 Paul Foster/Amelie & Friends; 5.2 Christopher Purchase; 5.3 Nigel Purchase; 5.4 Anne Scicluna/Christopher Purchase; 5.5 Iain McGowan

6.1 Chichester Camera Club/Chichester District Museum; 6. 2 Chichester District Museum; 6.3 Keith Fancy; 6.4 Ken Green; 6.5 Bernard Price literature; 6.6 Ken Green; 6. 7 Ken Green; 6. 8 John Templeton; 6.9 West Sussex Record Office; 6. 10 Ken Green; 6. 11 Rob Harmer; 6.12 Bernard Price Literature; 6.13 Ken Green; 6.14 West Sussex Record Office

7.1 Chichester City Council; 7.2 Chichester District Museum – Wally Dew Collection; 7.3 Alan H. J. Green; 7.4 Chichester Camera Club/Chichester District Museum; 7.5 Alan H. J. Green; 7.6 Ken Green; 7.7 Chichester Camera Club/Chichester District Museum; 7.8 C. Brewer & Sons Ltd; 7.9 C. Brewer & Sons Ltd; 7.10 Nigel Purchase; 7.11 Chichester District Council; 7.12 Andrew Berriman; 7.13 Alan H. J. Green

8.1 Ken Green; 8.2 Ken Green; 8.3 Ken Green; 8.4 Ken Green; 8.5 Richard Doman; 8.6 Chichester Camera Club/Chichester District Museum; 8.7 Jen Winghamx

9.1 Ken Green; 9.2 Ken Green; 9.3 John Dent; 9.4 John Dent; 9.5 Sheila Holden; 9.6 Vivian Meynell; 9.7 Vivian Meynell; 9.8 Vivian Meynell; 9.9 Clare at Moore & Tillyer Ltd; 9.10 Iain McGowan

10.1 Shirley Fox; 10.2 Shirley Fox; 10.3 David Goodman; 10.4 Shirley Fox; 10.5 Ken Green/Steve Griffith literature; 10.6 Nigel Purchase; 10.7 Nigel Purchase; 10.8 Nigel Purchase; 10.9 Iain McGowan; 10.10 Rosey Purchase; 10.11 John Shippam; 10.12 Ken Green; 10.13 Ken Green; 10.14 Sheila Hale; 10.15 Anon.

11.1 Keith & Julie Masters; 11.2 Richard Pailthorpe; 11.3 Keith & Julie Masters; 11.4 Pam Jupp; 11.5 Pam Jupp; 11.6 R. L. Austen

12.1 Sheila Hale/Kelly's 1930 Directory; 12.2 Sheila Hale/Kelly's 1930 Directory 12.3 Anon; 12.4 Iain McGowan; 12.5 Paul Willard; 12.6 West Sussex Record Office/ *Chichester Observer*

13.1 Timothy Bastow; 13.2 W. H. Smith; 13.3 Chichester Camera Club/Chichester District Museum; Iain McGowan; 13.4. Ken Green; 13. 5 Timothy Bastow; 13.6 Timothy Bastow; 13.7 Rosalind Bevis; 13.8 Ken Green; 13.9 Rosalind Bevis; 13.10 Ken Green; 13.11 Ken Green/Steve Griffith literature

OTTER MEMORIAL PAPERS
THE UNIVERSITY OF CHICHESTER
(General Editor: Professor Paul Foster)

Copies of papers may be obtained from the
University of Chichester, Chichester, West Sussex PO19 6PE
(omps@chi.ac.uk)

Number 12: *Flints, Ports, Otters & Threads: a Tribute to KM Elisabeth Murray 1909-98* (1998), pp. 112, illus. (2 b/w, 6 col.): Paul Foster *et al.*

Number 13: *Chichester Cathedral Spire - The Collapse (1861)* (2001), pp. 112, illus. (44 b/w, with coloured postcard - 2 images): John Atherton Bowen, Donald Buttress, Tessa Kelly, Victoria Rance, Gavin Stamp

Number 14: *Chagall Glass at Chichester and Tudeley July 2002; reprinted Nov 2002, 2004)*, pp. 104, illus. (3 b/w, 51 col.): Elizabeth Bewick, Tim Chilcott, Lawrence Ferlinghetti, Edward A. Hill, Robert Holtby, Alice Kettle, Michael Manktelow, June Osborne, Judith Peacock, Patrick Reyntiens, Pat Taylor, Gaynor Williams - with a preface by Jonathan Sacks

Number 15: *A Jewel in Stone: Chichester Market Cross 1501-2001* (2001; re-printed 2004), pp. 80, illus. (44 b/w): Judith Blake, Kenneth Child, Barry Fletcher, Andrew Foster, David Goodman, François Houtin, Francis Kyle, Keith Masters, Philip Morris, John Rankin, Anne Scicluna - with a preface by John Hind

Number 16: *Martina Thomas 1924-1995: Painter* (2003) – Chichester Modern Artists One, pp. 96, illus. (30 b/w, 59 col.): Judith Brooke, Paul Foster, David Goodman, Jeff Lowe, Elizabeth Spiro, Gaynor Williams

Number 17: *George Bell 1883-1958: The Prophetic Bishop* (2004), pp. 184, plus 10 colour plates: Ursula Baily, Philip Barrett, Adrian Carey, Andrew Chandler, Tom Devonshire Jones, Barbara Everard, Peter Graf, Martin Hüneke, Mary Joice, Eric Kemp, Hermine Lerbs, Tony Lloyd, Christa McKee-Lerbs,Michael Manktelow, Lancelot Mason, John Moorman, Roy Porter, James Radcliffe, Keith Robbins, Tonie Smith, Peter K. Walker, Giles Watson, Peter Wilkinson, Annemie de Witt

Number 18: *Chichester & the Arts 1944-2004* (2004), pp. 230, illus. (10 b/w, 86 col.): George Appleby, Brian Baxter, John Birch, Leon Bluestone, Pat Bowman, Marilyn Campbell, Josephine Gibson, David Goodman, Emma Goodman, Phil Hewitt, Peter Iden, Sarah Jones, Sharon-Michi Kusonoki, Kerry Manning, Simon Martin, Noel Osborne, David Page, Nigel Purchase, James Smith, Colin Stansfield Smith, Peter & Jean Thorpe, Ray Treagust, Alan Thurlow, Michael Waite, Gaynor Williams – with a preface by Patrick Garland

Number 19: *John Marsh of Chichester 1752-1828 – Gentleman, Musician, Composer, Writer* (2004), pp. 160. illus. (32 b/w, 11 col.): Barry Fletcher, Ian Graham-Jones, Ron Iden, Alison McCann, Timothy J. McCann, Patrick Moore, Nicholas Plumley, Martin Renshaw, Brian Robins, Emlyn Thomas, Alan Thurlow

Number 20: *David Goodman: Artist and Essayist* (2006) – Chichester Modern Artist Two pp. 72, illus. (22 b/w, 54 col.): Paul Foster, Gaynor Williams

Number 21: *Misericords in Sussex: a Photographic Record* (2007), pp. 92, illus. (169 sepia): Jean Barnes, Tony Barnes, Joy Whiting

Number 22: *Chichester Deans – Continuity, Commitment and Change at Chichester Cathedral 1902-2006* (2007): pp. 168, illus. (46 b/w, 8 col.): Ursula Baily, Geoffrey Barnard, Hilary Bryan-Brown, Paul Foster, Nicholas Frayling, Donald Gray, Robert Holtby, Tom Devonshire Jones, Michael Manktelow, Lancelot Mason, Chris Sparkes, John Treadgold, John Wyatt

Number 23: *Maureen Duke – Bookbinder, Teacher, Friend* (2008), pp. 112, illus. (42 b/w, 22 col.) with a postcard of Griffen Mill, Co. Sligo, and two sample handmade papers: Sonia Bradford, Liz Branigan, James Brockman, Edward Cheese, David Dorning, Wendy Egerton, David Graham, Elizabeth Neville, Gabrielle Fox, Freida Gumn,Teresa Januszonok, Sarah Jarrett-Kerr, Helen Kendall, Malcolm Lamb, Christine Laver Gibbs, Priscilla Noble-Mathews, Dominic Riley, Tracey Rowledge, Lori Sauer, Rob Shepherd, Angela Sutton, Elizabeth Webb, Gaynor Williams

Number 24: *George Bell Poems* (2008), pp. $x + 32 + 2$, with a portrait of George Bell, and a preface by Andrew Chandler; a numbered limited edition of 200 copies, being a facsimile of the edition published by Henrietta Bell in 1960

Number 25: *Richard of Chichester* (2009), pp. 124, illus. (12 b/w, 44 col.): Peter Atkinson, Anthony Cane, Jennie Gurney, Christopher Hassall, Philippa Hoskin, Philip Jackson, Mary Joice, David Jones, Tessa Kelly, Mary Medhurst, John Moorman, Rachel Moriarty, Kieron O'Brien, Richard Pfaff, Mike Stone - with a preface by John Hind

Number 26: *William Collins: Poet 1721-59* (2009), pp. 220, illus. (14 b/w, 2 col.): Diana Barsham, Trevor Brighton, Janet Carter, Andrew Chandler, Barbara Everard, Bill Hutchings, Zoe Kinsley, Adam Rounce, Duncan Salkeld, James Sambrook, John Wyatt

Number 27: *Chichester: The Palace and its Bishops – from the earliest times to 2001* (2011): Anthony Cane, Ken Carleton, Janet Carter, Andrew Chandler, Ruth Chavasse, Karen Coke, Sarah Foot, Andrew Foster, Ken Green, Philip Hind, Philippa Hoskin, Annemarie Nichols, Shaun Payne, Tim Tatton-Brown, Mark Taylor, Garth Turner, Peter Wilkinson, John Wyatt - with a preface by John Hind

Number 28: *From Orphan to Dean: a Biography of Robert Gregory (1819–1911) Dean of St Paul's (1891–1911)*, pp. 132, illus. (40 b/w, 7 col.): Sue Eastwood – with a preface by Graeme Knowles

Tradesman's cycle – displaying a true Baker's Dozen – adaptation courtesy Peter and Maureen Hancock